Magnetic Resonance Spectroscopy

ALLEN SERIES

WILEY SERIES IN PURE AND APPLIED SPECTROSCOPY

ADVISORY EDITOR: Harry C. Allen, Jr., National Bureau of Standards

Magnetic Resonance Spectroscopy

Harry G. Hecht
Los Alamos Scientific Laboratory
Los Alamos, New Mexico

JOHN WILEY & SONS, INC.   *New York London Sydney*

Preface

Probably never before in the history of science has so much highly precise and diverse information about the structure and properties of matter been obtained in a comparable span of time by any other method as has been accumulated within the last decade from microwave and radio-frequency spectroscopy.

This statement was made by Professor W. Gordy of Duke University in 1955 [*Discussions Faraday Soc.*, **19**, no. 14 (1955)], and the developments of the subsequent decade have been no less dramatic.

The motivations behind the writing of a book devoted to a subject for which there are already several books in existence require some explanation. Basically, they can be summed up as follows: there is no available survey of the field of magnetic resonance spectroscopy as a whole that is geared to the interests of a chemist and that is presented at a level appropriate for advanced undergraduate and beginning graduate students. With the flourishing of interest in this field in recent years, there is a need for a source of information that does not assume a high level of achievement in theoretical concepts. Many persons at this stage of their development find it necessary to rely on magnetic resonance data, either directly or indirectly, and it is hoped that this book will meet their needs.

Naturally, an appreciation of the importance of magnetic resonance parameters as it is related to chemical structure cannot be gained without the mastery of certain fundamentals. Those who are in any way associated with higher education in the physical sciences are well aware of the fact that the undergraduate chemistry curriculum is in a state of flux. Where it will end, or if it will ever end, no one really knows. But one thing is clear. At an early stage in their training students are being exposed to wave-mechanical concepts to some extent. An attempt has been made to rely only on a rudimentary knowledge in this regard, with the necessary extensions being discussed as required. My feeling of guilt for discussing here many concepts that were not familiar to me until much later in my own career is somewhat abated by a perusal of the material that pervades undergraduate textbooks of recent vintage.

This book is actually a somewhat enlarged and modified version of a set of lecture notes that was used for a one-semester course during the 1964–1965 school year at Texas Technological College. The class was composed primarily of beginning graduate students who represented all areas of chemistry. Thus rather diversified applications are presented in an attempt to meet the interests of such an eclectic group. The book is not comprehensive but is meant to be an introductory volume from which the student can gain some appreciation of what a magnetic resonance experiment is, how the various techniques are related, and in what way resonance parameters are used to infer structural information.

It is my pleasure to acknowledge the cooperation of those who granted permission to reproduce the various figures as cited in the captions. I am grateful to my graduate students at Texas Tech for the help they have given me in gathering and assimilating the information presented herein. A final revision of the manuscript was completed while I was in Australia as a Fulbright Advanced Research Scholar. I would like to express my gratitude to the Australian-American Educational Foundation and to the C.S.I.R.O. Division of Chemical Physics, which acted as the host institution. The comments of Dr. C. K. Coogan, Dr. I. D. Campbell, and particularly of Mr. S. N. Stuart, who read various parts of the manuscript, were very helpful and are greatly appreciated. Of course, I alone am responsible for any remaining errors. Last but not least, I should like to express my love and gratitude to my wife Glenda who tries (though sometimes in vain) to keep the children quiet while I work.

Melbourne, Victoria, Australia   HARRY G. HECHT
January 1967

Contents

Magnetic Resonance
Spectroscopy

I

Introduction

All electrons, and some nuclei, possess magnetic moments associated with an intrinsic or an orbital angular momentum, or both. In the event that there is an incomplete coupling of moments in the ion or molecule under consideration[1] these moments can interact with magnetic fields, both intrinsic and applied. These magnetic moments experience torques which tend to line them up in the magnetic field as if they were little bar magnets. The direct observation of such an alignment would naturally be very difficult. It is possible, however, to observe the absorption of energy from a magnetic field oscillating with a frequency in the radio or microwave region under appropriate conditions. This is the basic principle of the magnetic resonance method.

In such studies we are in essence using the electronic or nuclear moment as a magnetic probe to investigate the local magnetic effects within a molecule or ion. These are, in turn, a result of the electronic structure so that the magnetic resonance technique represents a very powerful tool for structural work. The fact that magnetic resonance spectrometers are fast becoming commonplace laboratory items is a testimonial to the usefulness of the method.

The first successful resonance experiment was of the paramagnetic type. It involved the iron group ions and was carried out by Zavoisky in Russia in 1944. This was soon followed by work in the United States by Cummerow and Halliday, but it is the British workers in the Clarendon Laboratory who are credited with the elucidation of many of the fundamental principles upon which our present understanding of electron resonance is based. It may seem strange at first to observe that the first experiments were not performed until the mid-1940's, when we consider that the basic concepts underlying such magnetic interactions were understood much earlier. One reason for this is the fact that microwave transmission and detection techniques were quite crude until the World

---

[1] This is always true of nuclei, and frequently of electrons.

1

War II period, during which time a great amount of technological effort was expended in their development.

It was not long after the first electron paramagnetic-resonance work that analogous nuclear resonances were also observed. This was achieved by two independent groups in 1945—one with Purcell at Harvard University and the other with Bloch at Stanford University. Purcell, Torrey, and Pound reported resonance absorption by protons in solid paraffin, while Bloch, Hansen, and Packard used a water sample. Although this marked the first observation of nuclear resonances in bulk samples, magnetic resonance experiments had been performed as early as the late 1930's by Rabi and several others using molecular beams. About this same time, Gorter had attempted to perform magnetic resonance in bulk samples without success.[1]

Nuclear magnetic resonance spectroscopy was used at first primarily by nuclear physicists for the accurate determination of nuclear moments. The first hint that these techniques might be useful to a chemist can probably be traced back to the work of Proctor and Yu, who together with Bloch noticed that the nuclear moment for nitrogen varies somewhat with the compound used for its determination. It was Arnold, Dharmatti, and Packard who first observed the three-line spectrum corresponding to the chemically inequivalent protons in ethyl alcohol in 1951, and following this event the nuclear magnetic resonance method moved very rapidly into the realm of chemistry.

Pure nuclear quadrupole resonance spectra were first observed in 1950 by Dehmelt and Krüger. Their experiments were performed using Cl^{35} resonance in solid *trans*-dichloroethylene.

Although we cannot consider all phases of magnetic resonance spectroscopy in depth in this small volume, we shall consider, following a discussion of the general theory, several of the specific methods that have been particularly useful in chemical structure analyses. Nuclear magnetic resonance (NMR), electron paramagnetic resonance (EPR), and nuclear quadrupole resonance (NQR) will be of primary concern, and we shall briefly review some of the double-resonance techniques which have proved to be very useful in recent years. Such techniques as ferromagnetic resonance and antiferromagnetic resonance have remained within the realm of solid-state physics for the most part, and will not be given specific consideration here.

---

[1] In early attempts (1936) Gorter tried to detect resonance absorption of energy by a calorimetric method. Later (1942), he looked for the anomalous dispersion which should accompany absorption, but apparently both these attempts owed their failure in large part to an unfortunate choice of materials.

2

Review of Quantum-
Mechanical Foundations

Before considering the behavior of various chemical species in the presence of magnetic fields, it will be necessary to consider the framework upon which our understanding of molecular structure is based. We review briefly here some of the essential concepts, and consider also the magnetic and electrical properties of electrons and nuclei which make them of interest in this regard. Although we can quite successfully account for many aspects of magnetic resonance spectroscopy in classical terms, it will be more profitable to rely primarily on the quantum-mechanical concepts mentioned here for much of our discussion.

2-1 OPERATORS, EIGENVALUES, AND EIGENFUNCTIONS

A quantum-mechanical operator[1] $\hat{Q}$ is defined in such a way that it performs some indicated operation on a given mathematical function. For example, $\hat{Q}$ might be taken to be $x \cdot$, d/dx, or $\int(\ )\,dx, \ldots$. If $\hat{Q}f(x) = qf(x)$, where q is a constant, then $f(x)$ is said to be the *eigenfunction* of the operator $\hat{Q}$, with *eigenvalue q*. All of quantum mechanics consists of finding the eigenfunctions for various operators. When we have constructed an appropriate operator, the eigenfunction can be used to describe the properties of a system. We proceed as follows. The *Hamiltonian operator* is constructed by writing the classical expression for the total energy of the system, in terms of *momenta* and coordinates, and by making the transformations

$$q_j \to q_j$$

$$p_j \to \frac{h}{2\pi i}\frac{\partial}{\partial q_j} = -i\hbar\frac{\partial}{\partial q_j}$$

[1] An operator is distinguished throughout this book from ordinary scalar and vector quantities by a circumflex.

Then the possible state functions Ψ are given by the solutions of the *Schrödinger equation*,

$$\hat{H}\Psi = -\frac{\hbar}{i}\frac{\partial\Psi}{\partial t} \tag{2-1}$$

where $\hat{H}$ is the appropriate Hamiltonian for the system. Equation 2–1 written out for the special case of a single particle is

$$-\frac{\hbar^2}{2m}\nabla^2\Psi + V(x, y, z, t)\Psi = -\frac{\hbar}{i}\frac{\partial\Psi}{\partial t}$$

where $V(x, y, z, t)$ is the potential function and $\nabla^2 \equiv \partial^2/\partial x^2 + \partial^2/\partial y^2 + \partial^2/\partial z^2$ is the *Laplacian operator*.

Usually, V is not a function of time, and stationary-state solutions are obtained. These are of the form

$$\Psi(q, t) = \psi(q)e^{-iEt/\hbar} \tag{2-2}$$

which, on insertion in Eq. 2–1 gives

$$\hat{H}\psi = E\psi \tag{2-3}$$

This is the Schrödinger equation not involving time.

The only observable values for a dynamical variable in an assembly of systems are those given by the eigenvalues satisfying the equation

$$\hat{Q}\varphi = q\varphi$$

where $\hat{Q}$ is the appropriate operator for that variable, and φ is any well-behaved eigenfunction of $\hat{Q}$ (single-valued, continuous, and integrable). The average value, or *expectation value*, of many measurements of a dynamical variable for an assembly of systems is given by

$$\bar{q} = \frac{\int \psi^*\hat{Q}\psi \, d\tau}{\int \psi^*\psi \, d\tau} \equiv \frac{\langle \psi | \hat{Q} | \psi \rangle}{\langle \psi | \psi \rangle} \tag{2-4}$$

where the volume element is $d\tau$ and the integration is carried out over all space. Although the second way of writing Eq. 2–4 was introduced by Dirac for quite a different reason, we can regard it as merely a simplified notation for our purposes. With the wave function ψ normalized, so that $\psi^*\psi$ can be interpreted in terms of a probability density

$$\langle \psi | \psi \rangle = 1 \tag{2-5}$$

2–2   APPROXIMATION METHODS

The few simple systems for which exact quantum-mechanical solutions are possible do not apply to many actual situations of chemical interest, and we must rely on approximation methods to determine wave functions as best we can. Two are commonly employed by chemists: the variation method and the perturbation method.

Variation Method

The basis of the variation method is the following theorem which can be readily proved. If ψ is any well-behaved function which is normalized, and if the lowest eigenvalue of the operator $\hat{H}$ is E_0, then

$$\langle\psi|\,\hat{H}\,|\psi\rangle \geq E_0 \qquad (2\text{-}6)$$

This important result, in other words, states that any arbitrary wave function used to evaluate the energy by means of Eq. 2–4 leads to a result which is either greater than or equal to the true ground-state energy of the system. This seems reasonable in view of the fact that we are attempting to find a description of a physical situation in terms of our mathematical formalism. One of the fundamental characteristics of any system is that it will tend to be in the lowest energy state possible, so that it is inconceivable that we could mathematically construct an energy state which is better than any mother nature could devise!

Armed with the variation theorem, we have a powerful method of finding approximate solutions. If we minimize the energy with respect to several parameters occurring in the wave function, we obtain the *best* approximation to the ground-state energy which is possible for a wave function *of that particular form*. The variation theorem assures us that we can never get an energy that is too low by this procedure.

One of the most commonly used trial solutions for the variation method is constructed by taking the wave function to be a linear combination of eigenfunctions of some particular operator. We write this as

$$\psi = \sum_{i=1}^{n} c_i \varphi_i \qquad (2\text{-}7)$$

The expectation value of the energy, from Eq. 2–4, is

$$\bar{E} = \frac{\left\langle \sum_{i=1}^{n} c_i\varphi_i \,\middle|\, \hat{H} \,\middle|\, \sum_{i=1}^{n} c_i\varphi_i \right\rangle}{\left\langle \sum_{i=1}^{n} c_i\varphi_i \,\middle|\, \sum_{i=1}^{n} c_i\varphi_i \right\rangle}$$

As a matter of convenience we introduce the notation

$$H_{ij} = \langle\varphi_i|\,\hat{H}\,|\varphi_j\rangle \qquad (2\text{-}8a)$$
$$S_{ij} = \langle\varphi_i\,|\,\varphi_j\rangle \qquad (2\text{-}8b)$$

and, for reasons which will be obvious later, we refer to these quantities as *matrix elements*. Fortunately, it always happens that $H_{ij} = H_{ji}$ for the operators of quantum-mechanical interest, and $S_{ij} = S_{ji}$. Furthermore, we can always construct wave functions in such a way that they are real, for which $c_i^* = c_i$. Then, using the foregoing notation, the energy can be written

$$\bar{E} = \frac{\sum\limits_{j,k=1}^{n} c_j c_k H_{jk}}{\sum\limits_{j,k=1}^{n} c_j c_k S_{jk}} \tag{2-9}$$

$\bar{E}$ is minimized with respect to each of the coefficients c_i by differentiation of Eq. 2–9 with respect to each c_i and setting $\partial \bar{E}/\partial c_i = 0$. The resulting equations can then be solved for the c_i's. The differentiation of Eq. 2–9 gives

$$\bar{E}\sum_{k=1}^{n} c_k S_{ik} + \bar{E}\sum_{j=1}^{n} c_j S_{ji} = \sum_{k=1}^{n} c_k H_{ik} + \sum_{j=1}^{n} c_j H_{ji}$$

which, because of the symmetry of H_{ij} and S_{ij} with respect to a change in the order of the subscripts, reduces to

$$\bar{E}\sum_{j=1}^{n} c_j S_{ij} = \sum_{j=1}^{n} c_j H_{ij}$$

or

$$\sum_{j=1}^{n}(H_{ij} - \bar{E}S_{ij})c_j = 0 \tag{2-10}$$

We have an equation just like Eq. 2–10 for each and every value of i from 1 to n. Written out, they appear as follows:

$$(H_{11} - \bar{E}S_{11})c_1 + (H_{12} - \bar{E}S_{12})c_2 + \cdots + (H_{1n} - \bar{E}S_{1n})c_n = 0$$
$$(H_{21} - \bar{E}S_{21})c_1 + (H_{22} - \bar{E}S_{22})c_2 + \cdots + (H_{2n} - \bar{E}S_{2n})c_n = 0$$
$$\cdot$$
$$\cdot \tag{2-11}$$
$$\cdot$$
$$(H_{n1} - \bar{E}S_{n1})c_1 + (H_{n2} - \bar{E}S_{n2})c_2 + \cdots + (H_{nn} - \bar{E}S_{nn})c_n = 0$$

In more compact matrix notation, these equations can be written

$$\mathbf{Hc} = \bar{E}\mathbf{Sc}$$

where $\mathbf{H}$ and $\mathbf{S}$ are $n \times n$ square matrices whose elements were previously defined, and $\mathbf{c}$ is a $n \times 1$ column matrix which is frequently referred to as the *eigenvector*. Equations 2–11 are called *secular equations*. They are homogeneous and linear, and can be readily solved for the coefficients c_i

by using such techniques as Cramer's rule, which, it will be recalled, states that the solutions are given by

$$c_1 = \frac{D_1}{D} \qquad c_2 = \frac{D_2}{D} \qquad c_3 = \frac{D_3}{D} \qquad \text{etc.}$$

where D is the determinant of the coefficients and D_i is derived from it by replacing the ith column by the constant factors. In this case, however, the constant factors are all zeros, so that every $D_i = 0$. This constitutes a solution, but it is a trivial one of no interest to us.

The only nontrivial solutions that can be obtained are found by setting $D = 0$, which leads to indeterminate forms for the c_i's. We must thus solve

$$\begin{vmatrix} (H_{11} - \bar{E}S_{11}) & (H_{12} - \bar{E}S_{12}) & \cdots & (H_{1n} - \bar{E}S_{1n}) \\ (H_{21} - \bar{E}S_{21}) & (H_{22} - \bar{E}S_{22}) & \cdots & (H_{2n} - \bar{E}S_{2n}) \\ \vdots & & & \\ (H_{n1} - \bar{E}S_{n1}) & (H_{n2} - \bar{E}S_{n2}) & \cdots & (H_{nn} - \bar{E}S_{nn}) \end{vmatrix} = 0 \quad (2\text{-}12)$$

which is known as the *secular determinant*. The secular determinant leads to an nth-degree polynomial in $\bar{E}$ when expanded, so there will be n values of $\bar{E}$ which satisfy the foregoing condition. Actually there are only $n - 1$ secular equations which are independent when $\bar{E}$ is chosen so that the secular determinant is satisfied. Thus, only $n - 1$ of Eqs. 2–11 can be used, so that we solve for a set of ratios, $c_2/c_1, c_3/c_1, \ldots, c_n/c_1$, corresponding to each eigenvalue $\bar{E}$. The associated eigenvector is completely determined by including the normalization condition.[1] The eigenvector is interpreted as defining the relative contributions of each of the wave functions φ_i, which define the n-dimensional vector space of which the resultant energy state is composed.

Perturbation Method

The perturbation method is useful for finding the solution of problems whose Hamiltonian differs very little from that of a system for which the solution is known. We write

$$\hat{H} = \hat{H}_0 + \hat{H}' \qquad (2\text{-}13)$$

where it is assumed that $\hat{H}' \ll \hat{H}_0$ and that the solutions of

$$\hat{H}_0 \psi_n{}^0 = E_n^{(0)} \psi_n{}^0 \qquad (2\text{-}14)$$

---

[1] Another way of saying this is that we can only solve for n unknowns by using the n secular equations. All $n + 1$ unknowns, $c_1, c_2, c_3, \ldots, c_n$ and $\bar{E}$, can be determined by inclusion of the additional Eq. 2–5.

are known (the so-called zeroth-order solutions). As a next approximation, it is assumed that the effect of the perturbation on the wave function
is very small. We shall as a matter of fact assume that the wave function,
and consequently the probability density, is unaltered by the perturbation
to this degree of approximation. The zeroth-order energy as given by
Eq. 2–14 is

$$E_n^{(0)} = \frac{1}{\psi_n^{0}} \hat{H}_0 \psi_n^{0}$$

and, by analogy, we write for the energy of the perturbed system,

$$E_n = \frac{1}{\psi_n^{0}} \hat{H} \psi_n^{0} = \frac{1}{\psi_n^{0}} (\hat{H}_0 + \hat{H}') \psi_n^{0} \tag{2–15}$$

Because ψ_n^{0} is no longer an exact eigenfunction of the Hamiltonian, the
energy calculated in this way will no longer be exactly constant but will
vary somewhat with the coordinates. Thus, we shall calculate the average
perturbed energy by integrating the energy weighted by the probability
density over all configuration space. This gives

$$\bar{E} = \frac{\langle \psi_n^{0} | E_n | \psi_n^{0} \rangle}{\langle \psi_n^{0} | \psi_n^{0} \rangle} = \left\langle \psi_n^{0} \left| \frac{1}{\psi_n^{0}} (\hat{H}_0 + \hat{H}') \psi_n^{0} \right| \psi_n^{0} \right\rangle$$

where it has been assumed that ψ_n^{0} is normalized. Using Eq. 2–14, we
obtain

$$\bar{E} = \left\langle \psi_n^{0} \left| \frac{1}{\psi_n^{0}} (E_n^{(0)} \psi_n^{0} + \hat{H}' \psi_n^{0}) \right| \psi_n^{0} \right\rangle$$

$$= E_n^{(0)} + \langle \psi_n^{0} | \hat{H}' | \psi_n^{0} \rangle \tag{2–16}$$

This is the energy of the system, correct to *first order*. We note that it
involves a knowledge of the zeroth-order wave functions only.

Actually, the foregoing result is but the first term in a series expansion.
Higher-order terms lead to additional corrections in which the alteration
of the wave function by the perturbation can no longer be ignored.
Correct to second order,

$$\bar{E} = E_n^{(0)} + E_n^{(1)} + E_n^{(2)} \tag{2–17}$$

with

$$E_n^{(1)} = \langle \psi_n^{0} | \hat{H}' | \psi_n^{0} \rangle \qquad E_n^{(2)} = \sum_{m \neq n} \frac{\langle \psi_n^{0} | \hat{H}' | \psi_m^{0} \rangle \langle \psi_m^{0} | \hat{H}' | \psi_n^{0} \rangle}{E_n^{0} - E_m^{0}}$$

$$\tag{2–17a}$$

The perturbed wave function, correct to this same order, is

$$|\psi_n\rangle = |\psi_n^{0}\rangle + \sum_{m \neq n} \frac{\langle \psi_m^{0} | \hat{H}' | \psi_n^{0} \rangle}{E_n^{(0)} - E_m^{(0)}} |\psi_m^{0}\rangle \tag{2–18}$$

Second-order perturbation theory thus involves a knowledge of all the excited states of the unperturbed system. Unfortunately, this information is not usually available for molecules.

It might be noted that the first-order perturbation terms are just the diagonal elements of a complete perturbation matrix. The second-order terms involve off-diagonal elements along a single row and column, weighted by the energy difference. Continuing, we ultimately would, in principle, solve the complete matrix. In practice we seldom go past second-order corrections.

2–3 VALENCE THEORY

There are several methods we can use to discuss the structure of molecules. Historically, the first to be developed following the introduction of wave mechanical principles in the 1920's was the valence-bond method. This was an outgrowth of the Heitler-London treatment of the hydrogen molecule, and explicitly incorporated the concept of the localized electron-pair bond. This method remained popular for quite some time, but then seemingly gave way to the molecular-orbital method, which, although offering no advantages in the calculation of good ground-state wave functions, gained favor because the excited states are incorporated in the treatment in a natural way, which makes it more useful for the interpretation of the usual spectroscopic data. Magnetic resonance involves the excited states in an indirect way only, however, and both methods have proved to be very useful in this connection. As is well known, each has its limitations, but the two methods do converge to identical results if higher-order contributions are included.[1]

Although each of these methods is in principle applicable to any chemical-structure problem, a more useful approach has been found for the treatment of complex ions that has been quite thoroughly exploited in recent years. This is the ligand-field theory, which is distinguished

---

[1] Basically, the distinction is this: For a homopolar bond, the valence-bond method includes with equal probability the placement of electrons 1 and 2 on atoms a and b, $\psi_{vb} = \psi_a(1)\psi_b(2) + \psi_a(2)\psi_b(1)$, while the molecular-orbital method assumes a wave function of the type, $\psi_{mo} = [\psi_a(1) + \psi_b(1)][\psi_a(2) + \psi_b(2)]$, which again shows the equal probability of an electron being associated with atoms a and b. The molecular-orbital theory deals with one-electron orbitals, however, with the appropriate total wave function being given by their product. Expansion of the latter shows that ionic terms of types $\psi_a(1)\psi_a(2)$ and $\psi_b(1)\psi_b(2)$ are included on an equal footing with covalent terms, which surely overemphasizes their contribution. The complete omission of these ionic terms in the valence-bond wave function is equally incorrect. The compromise comes about by introducing excited states into the ground-state wave function in the molecular-orbital calculation (configuration interaction) or by the inclusion of an ionic term $\lambda[\psi_a(1)\psi_a(2) + \psi_b(1)\psi_b(2)]$ in the valence-bond wave function, where $\lambda \ll 1$.

from its predecessor, the crystal-field theory, by inclusion of the effects of orbital mixing between the metal and ligand atoms. Although there are some limitations, the ligand-field method, in which attention is focused primarily on the behavior of the unfilled d and f orbitals in various environments, is very useful. However, it must be recognized that it is ultimately just a first approximation to a complete quantum-mechanical solution.

These three methods are widely used to treat chemical valence problems, and an understanding of their basic tenets is essential to our subsequent discussions. For this reason a brief discussion of the characteristic features is included here. They will hereafter be referred to as v.b. (valence-bond), m.o. (molecular-orbital), and l.f. (ligand-field) methods.

Valence-Bond Theory

As is well known, all electrons behave as though they were spinning on their own axes, with quantized z-components of angular momentum given by $+\frac{1}{2}$ or $-\frac{1}{2}$ (in units of $\hbar$).[1] We represent the wave function for spin $+\frac{1}{2}$ by α, and that for spin $-\frac{1}{2}$ by β. Each electron in a molecule must be assigned either an α or a β spin, together with an orbital defined by the spacial coordinates. There are numerous ways of making such assignments. All permutations of electrons are possible, with the Pauli exclusion principle requiring that the wave function be antisymmetric, i.e., it must change sign for an odd number of electron interchanges and retain the same algebraic sign for an even number. This restriction is conveniently incorporated by writing the wave function in the form of a *Slater determinant:*

$$\psi = \frac{1}{\sqrt{n!}} \begin{vmatrix} \psi_a(1)\alpha(1) & \psi_b(1)\beta(1) & \cdots & \psi_n(1)\alpha(1) \\ \psi_a(2)\alpha(2) & \psi_b(2)\beta(2) & \cdots & \psi_n(2)\alpha(2) \\ \cdot & & & \\ \cdot & & & \\ \cdot & & & \\ \psi_a(n)\alpha(n) & \psi_b(n)\beta(n) & \cdots & \psi_n(n)\alpha(n) \end{vmatrix} \qquad (2\text{--}19)$$

$1/\sqrt{n!}$ is a normalization factor, and only one of many possible assignments of spin with spacial orbitals is illustrated in Eq. 2–19, i.e., α with ψ_a, β with ψ_b, ... Note that if Eq. 2–19 were written in such a way that two or more electrons occupied the same spacial *and* spin orbitals (all quantum numbers the same), the configuration would vanish by the usual rules for expanding determinants.

These matters are discussed in more detail in Sec. 2–4.

The essence of the v.b. method is the construction of *bond functions* which describe particular pairing schemes for the bonding electrons. Let us illustrate this by consideration of a specific case—the π-electron structure of benzene. The six electrons (one per carbon atom) which remain after the σ bonds are formed occupy $2p_\pi$ orbitals and are available for the formation of delocalized bonds (see Fig. 2–1).

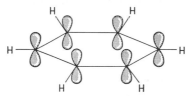

Fig. 2–1 $2p_\pi$ atomic orbitals of benzene.

The most obvious pairing schemes to consider are those which lead to the Kekulé structures:

There are many others, however, of which the following are examples:

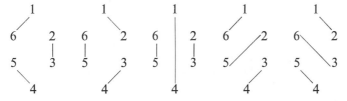

The bond function for each of these structures can be written out in terms of the abovementioned Slater determinants, and in general there will be many determinants which satisfy the bonding scheme. Structure *a*, for example, requires only that there be an α-β pair, or spin correlation, between atoms 1 and 6, 2 and 3, and 4 and 5, and there are many determinants which have this feature.

We quickly find that many of these bond functions can be expressed as linear combinations of others. A very convenient device was conceived by Rumer for the construction of a complete set, in terms of which all others can be expressed. We construct a circle with the atoms numbered around it, and connect them in pairs, *with no lines crossing:*

Such a set of bond structures is called the *canonical set,* and it can be shown that there are

$$\frac{n!}{(n/2)! \, [(n/2) + 1]!}$$
(2–20)

structures for an *n*-electron problem. In our case, the canonical set is obviously composed of the two Kekulé structures, *a* and *b,* together with the three Dewar structures, *c, d,* and *e.*

The calculation of the matrix elements of $\hat{H}$ (Eq. 2–8*a*) for the bond structures, which are in turn expressed in terms of the Slater determinants, turns out to be a very tedious problem the details of which need not concern us here. Systematic rules for their evaluation have been worked out, notably by Eyring and Kimball and by Pauling, which are simple to apply. One constructs a *superposition diagram* by combination of the π-bonding schemes for two different structures. For example, the *b-d* superposition diagram is

b-d

There are two closed contours (one is a line, actually, in this case), which are spoken of as *islands.* The matrix elements can be written as

$$H_{ij} = \frac{1}{2^{[(n/2)-x_{ij}]}} \left(Q + \sum_{k \neq l} P_{kl} I_{kl} \right)$$

$$S_{ij} = \frac{1}{2^{[(n/2)-x_{ij}]}}$$
(2–21)

n, as previously mentioned, is the number of electrons, and x_{ij} is the number of islands. Q and I_{kl} are integrals over the individual spacial orbitals which make up the Slater determinants (Eq. 2–19). The first, Q, is known as the *Coulomb integral,*

$$Q = \iint \psi_i(1)\psi_j(2)\hat{H}\psi_i(1)\psi_j(2) \, d\tau_1 \, d\tau_2$$
(2–22)

The second, the *exchange integral,* is defined as

$$I_{ij} = \iint \psi_i(1)\psi_j(2)\hat{H}\psi_i(2)\psi_j(1) \, d\tau_1 \, d\tau_2$$
(2–23)

P_{kl} is the *exchange factor,* which is $+1$ for orbitals in the same island separated by an odd number of bonds, -2 for orbitals in the same island separated by an even number of bonds, and $-\frac{1}{2}$ for orbitals in different islands.[1] As an example, the b-d matrix elements are

$$H_{bd} = \tfrac{1}{2}[Q + I_{12} + I_{16} + I_{25} + I_{56} + I_{34} - 2I_{15} - 2I_{26}$$
$$- \tfrac{1}{2}I_{13} - \tfrac{1}{2}I_{14} - \tfrac{1}{2}I_{23} - \tfrac{1}{2}I_{24} - \tfrac{1}{2}I_{35} - \tfrac{1}{2}I_{45} - \tfrac{1}{2}I_{36} - \tfrac{1}{2}I_{46}]$$

and

$$S_{bd} = \tfrac{1}{2}$$

We can construct a secular determinant based upon a linear combination of bond functions (see Eq. 2–7):

$$\Psi = c_a\psi_a + c_b\psi_b + c_c\psi_c + c_d\psi_d + c_e\psi_e$$

Only the bond functions corresponding to the canonical structures are included because the addition of any linear combination of them introduces nothing new. We evaluate the matrix elements as above, assuming that the exchange interaction between all atoms except nearest neighbors is sufficiently small so that it can be neglected. Using q to represent the exchange energy I (Eq. 2–23) between nearest neighbors, we get,

$$\begin{vmatrix}
[(Q-\bar{E})+\tfrac{3}{2}q] & [\tfrac{1}{4}(Q-\bar{E})+\tfrac{3}{4}q] & [\tfrac{1}{2}(Q-\bar{E})+\tfrac{3}{4}q] & [\tfrac{1}{2}(Q-\bar{E})+\tfrac{3}{4}q] & [\tfrac{1}{2}(Q-\bar{E})+\tfrac{3}{4}q] \\
[\tfrac{1}{4}(Q-\bar{E})+\tfrac{3}{4}q] & [(Q-\bar{E})+\tfrac{3}{2}q] & [\tfrac{1}{2}(Q-\bar{E})+\tfrac{3}{4}q] & [\tfrac{1}{2}(Q-\bar{E})+\tfrac{3}{4}q] & [\tfrac{1}{2}(Q-\bar{E})+\tfrac{3}{4}q] \\
[\tfrac{1}{2}(Q-\bar{E})+\tfrac{3}{4}q] & [\tfrac{1}{2}(Q-\bar{E})+\tfrac{3}{4}q] & [(Q-\bar{E})] & [\tfrac{1}{4}(Q-\bar{E})+\tfrac{3}{4}q] & [\tfrac{1}{4}(Q-E)+\tfrac{3}{4}q] \\
[\tfrac{1}{2}(Q-\bar{E}+\tfrac{3}{4}q] & [\tfrac{1}{2}(Q-\bar{E})+\tfrac{3}{4}q] & [\tfrac{1}{4}(Q-\bar{E})+\tfrac{3}{4}q] & [(Q-\bar{E}] & [\tfrac{1}{4}(Q-\bar{E})+\tfrac{3}{4}q] \\
[\tfrac{1}{2}(Q-\bar{E})+\tfrac{3}{4}q] & [\tfrac{1}{2}(Q-\bar{E})+\tfrac{3}{4}q] & [\tfrac{1}{4}(Q-\bar{E})+\tfrac{3}{4}q] & [\tfrac{1}{4}(Q-\bar{E})+\tfrac{3}{4}q] & [(Q-\bar{E})]
\end{vmatrix} = 0$$

The lowest root of this equation is found to be (Q and q are both negative),

$$\bar{E} = Q + 2.6q$$

A comparison of this value with the energy of a single Kekulé structure,

$$\bar{E} = Q + 1.5q$$

indicates that we should attribute a quantity of energy, $1.1q$, to resonance stabilization. From thermodynamic considerations, it is found that this amounts to about 40 kcal/mole in the case of benzene. If structures a and b alone are considered, the energy is found to be

$$\bar{E} = Q + 2.4q$$

[1] Note that what we are doing is forcing particular electrons to be of bonding or antibonding character by considering resonance between two structures. If we, for example, start with atom 1 in structure b and assign it an α spin, then the electron on atom 2 must be β. Comparing this with structure d indicates that atom 5 must then have an α electron, which in turn forces atom 6 to have an electron of β spin. Bonding interactions (spins paired) lead to an interaction energy with a $+1$ coefficient for the exchange integral and antibonding interactions (spins parallel) are characterized by a -2 coefficient. A random orientation of spins, which is allowed for orbitals in different islands, leads to a value $-\tfrac{1}{2}$.

so it is concluded that about

$$\frac{2.4q - 1.5q}{2.6q - 1.5q} \, 100 = 82\%$$

of the stabilization is due to the Kekulé structures. An evaluation of the wave function as outlined in Sec. 2–1 leads to

$$\Psi = 0.6244(\psi_a + \psi_b) + 0.2710(\psi_c + \psi_d + \psi_e)$$

Since the probability of any structure is proportional to the square of its coefficient in the normalized wave function, it is found that the probability of Kekulé-type configurations is about 0.78, compared with about 0.22 for the combined Dewar-type configurations.

Excited electronic states can be handled in the v.b. theory also, but they will generally involve higher multiplicities (less spin pairing) and will be considerably more difficult to handle.

Molecular-Orbital Theory

The distinguishing feature of the m.o. theory is the construction of one-electron orbitals which are not necessarily localized between pairs of atoms. Again, the delocalized π-bond structure of benzene will be used to illustrate the method. The m.o. wave function is usually assumed to be of the l.c.a.o. type (linear combination of atomic orbitals), and we write

$$\Psi = \sum_{i=1}^{6} c_i \varphi_i$$

where φ_i represents a $2p_\pi$ atomic orbital located on carbon atom i. Straightforward application of the variation method leads to a sixth-order secular determinant (Eq. 2–12), whose matrix elements must be evaluated in terms of the abovementioned $2p$ carbon orbitals. Their evaluation proceeds with great difficulty, however, because the Hamiltonian operator must be constructed in such a way as to incorporate the *effective* field in which the electrons move. This not only includes the nuclear framework but also the σ-bonding electrons and atomic inner shells as well. Thus, we again resort to the use of parameters to represent the necessary integrals.

A simple means of specifying these parameters was suggested by Hückel, and is widely used today for semiquantitative work. The *overlap integrals* S_{ij} are taken to be zero for $i \neq j$, and unity for $i = j$. In other words, the φ_i functions are assumed to be orthogonal and normalized.

H_{ij} is represented by the parameter α for all $i = j$, and is known as the *Coulomb integral*. With i and j chosen in such a way that H_{ij} represents the interaction of an electron between neighboring atoms, a parameter β is assigned, which is referred to as the *resonance integral*. The resonance interaction is assumed to be negligible for all combinations of atoms which are not directly bonded.

With the use of these approximations, the secular determinant is reduced to

$$
\begin{vmatrix}
\alpha - \bar{E} & \beta & 0 & 0 & 0 & \beta \\
\beta & \alpha - \bar{E} & \beta & 0 & 0 & 0 \\
0 & \beta & \alpha - \bar{E} & \beta & 0 & 0 \\
0 & 0 & \beta & \alpha - \bar{E} & \beta & 0 \\
0 & 0 & 0 & \beta & \alpha - \bar{E} & \beta \\
\beta & 0 & 0 & 0 & \beta & \alpha - \bar{E}
\end{vmatrix} = 0
$$

The roots of this and similar equations are conveniently expressed in the form

$$
\bar{E} = \alpha + 2\beta \cos \frac{2\pi j}{n} \tag{2-24}
$$

where n is the number of electrons involved (six in this case), and j takes on values between 1 and n. The roots turn out to be

$$
\bar{E}_1 = \alpha + 2\beta
$$
$$
\bar{E}_2 = \alpha + \beta
$$
$$
\bar{E}_3 = \alpha + \beta
$$
$$
\bar{E}_4 = \alpha - \beta
$$
$$
\bar{E}_5 = \alpha - \beta
$$
$$
\bar{E}_6 = \alpha - 2\beta
$$

It will be noted that there are twofold degeneracies involving states 2 and 3, and 4 and 5. Since α and β are negative quantities, the states have been listed in order of increasing energy. The actual values of α and β, which are found by spectroscopic and thermodynamic considerations are $\alpha \approx -35$ kcal/mole and $\beta \approx -20$ kcal/mole.

The wave functions can be found by putting these values of the energy back into the secular equations, as previously described, and normalizing the result. We obtain the following:

$$\Psi_1 = \frac{1}{\sqrt{6}} (\varphi_1 + \varphi_2 + \varphi_3 + \varphi_4 + \varphi_5 + \varphi_6)$$

$$\Psi_{2,3} = \begin{cases} \dfrac{1}{\sqrt{12}} (2\varphi_1 + \varphi_2 - \varphi_3 - 2\varphi_4 - \varphi_5 + \varphi_6) \\ \dfrac{1}{\sqrt{12}} (\varphi_1 + 2\varphi_2 + \varphi_3 - \varphi_4 - 2\varphi_5 - \varphi_6) \end{cases}$$

$$\Psi_{4,5} = \begin{cases} \dfrac{1}{\sqrt{12}} (2\varphi_1 - \varphi_2 - \varphi_3 + 2\varphi_4 - \varphi_5 - \varphi_6) \\ \dfrac{1}{\sqrt{12}} (\varphi_1 - 2\varphi_2 + \varphi_3 + \varphi_4 - 2\varphi_5 + \varphi_6) \end{cases}$$

$$\Psi_6 = \frac{1}{\sqrt{6}} (\varphi_1 - \varphi_2 + \varphi_3 - \varphi_4 + \varphi_5 - \varphi_6)$$

It is interesting to note the way the sign alternates in these various states as we proceed around the ring. Ψ_1 corresponds to a completely symmetric additive combination of the atomic orbitals for which the molecular orbital is of the form shown in Fig. 2–2a. Ψ_2 and Ψ_3, which differ only in phase, are of the form shown in Fig. 2–2b.

The remaining states can be similarly pictured, it being observed that the number of *nodes*[1] in the wave function increases with the energy.

The complete specification of the one-electron molecular orbitals requires that the electron be assigned a spin state also. For the time being, we can neglect this and put electrons into the π-orbital structure we have just calculated assuming a twofold degeneracy for each of the states. There results for the benzene molecule the diagram shown in Fig. 2–3.

To this degree of approximation, the π-electron energy is $2(\alpha + 2\beta) + 4(\alpha + \beta) = 6\alpha + 8\beta$. It is of interest to consider what result is obtained for a single Kekulé structure. Each $2p_\pi$ electron is in this case regarded as associated with a single adjacent electron, so that the appropriate molecular orbital is a linear combination of atomic orbitals for two adjacent carbon atoms only, e.g., φ_1 with φ_2, φ_3 with φ_4, etc. The energy for a single electron is then obtained by solution of any one of three

---

[1] A node may be alternatively viewed as a point in space where the wave function changes sign or where the electron probability density vanishes.

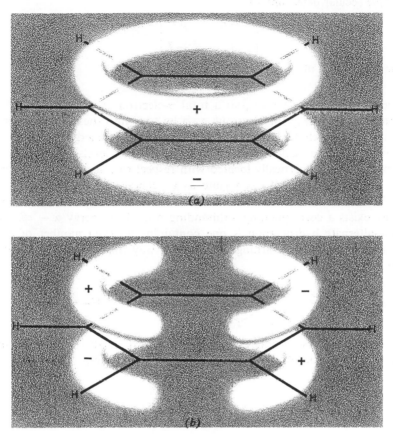

Fig. 2-2   (a) Lowest π orbital of benzene; (b) second π orbital of benzene.

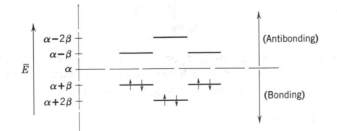

Fig. 2-3   Energy-level diagram for the π orbitals of benzene.

simple secular determinants

$$\begin{vmatrix} \alpha - \bar{E} & \beta \\ \beta & \alpha - \bar{E} \end{vmatrix} = 0$$

the lowest root of which is

$$\bar{E} = \alpha + \beta$$

There are three such roots, so a total π-electron energy of $6\alpha + 6\beta$ is obtained by placing the electrons, two by two, into these lowest energy states. We conclude that the resonance stabilization energy is 2β.

It might have been noticed that the calculated levels in the case of benzene are symmetrically located with respect to α as a reference point on an energy scale. We can state as a general rule for *even-alternate* hydrocarbons that, for every bonding orbital with energy $\alpha + x\beta$ ($x > 0$), there exists a corresponding antibonding orbital of energy $\alpha - x\beta$. An even-alternate hydrocarbon is one containing an even number of conjugated carbon atoms arranged in such a way that one can star every other atom:

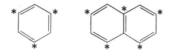

Not all species of interest can be classified in this way, however. Toluene, for example, is an *odd-alternate* hydrocarbon,

and molecules containing odd-membered rings, such as azulene,

are *nonalternate*. Odd-alternate hydrocarbons have the same symmetry of bonding and antibonding orbitals as even-alternate hydrocarbons, except that there is an additional nonbonding orbital.

Ligand-Field Theory

As previously mentioned, l.f. theory is primarily concerned with the effect of different environments on the d and f orbitals. These subshells, because of their partially filled nature, endow the transition and inner-transition elements with characteristic spectroscopic and magnetic properties with which we will be concerned. As a starting point, we consider the coordination sphere of a given metal ion as providing an effective electric field which serves to remove the degeneracy of the d and f orbitals. The naive assumption is usually made that the ligands can be regarded as point charges or dipoles in this regard, and if we neglect the mixing of metal and ligand orbitals (covalent bonding), the crystal-field potential will have to satisfy Laplace's equation

$$\nabla^2 V_c = 0 \tag{2-25}$$

A crystal-field potential can be quite readily constructed which fulfills this condition. Such a potential is treated as a perturbation on the hydrogenlike orbitals of the free ion. We will sketch the main features of the calculation of the splitting of the d levels by an octahedral crystal field, omitting the more or less laborious details.

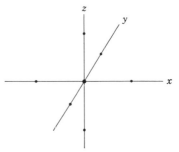

Fig. 2-4   Octahedral coordination of a metal ion.

Consider a metal ion to be placed at the origin of coordinates, with ligands at equal distances along the $\pm x$-, $\pm y$-, and $\pm z$-axes (see Fig. 2-4). These ligands can be regarded as either point electrical charges (for negative ligands such as F^- or Cl^-) or point dipoles (for polar ligands such as H_2O or NH_3). In either case, the interaction will be predominated by the attraction of the metal ion for the negative charges, and we can write for the interaction potential,

$$V_c = \sum_i V_i = -\sum_i \frac{Ze^2}{r_i}$$

where Z is the effective metal charge, in units of e, and r_i is the metal-ligand distance. It is convenient to write this in somewhat different form for actual calculations. The *spherical harmonics*,[1]

$$Y_l^m = P_l^{|m|}(\cos\theta)e^{im\phi}$$
$$= \frac{(-1)^l}{2^l l!}\sqrt{\frac{(2l+1)(l-|m|)!}{4\pi(l+|m|)!}}\sin^{|m|}\theta\frac{d^{l+|m|}\sin^{2l}\theta}{(d\cos\theta)^{l+|m|}}e^{im\phi} \tag{2-26}$$

form a complete orthogonal set of functions, so that any arbitrary function can be expressed in terms of a linear combination of them. In our case,

[1] Although we usually need not be concerned with the specific form of these functions, they are extremely important, and we will find it necessary to refer to them in other connections as well. Problems in which there are central forces will in general involve the spherical harmonics, so that they play a central role in many quantum-mechanical problems.

the crystal-field potential is simply,

$$V_c = A_0{}^0 Y_0{}^0 + A_4{}^0 Y_4{}^0 + \sqrt{\tfrac{5}{14}} A_4{}^0 (Y_4{}^4 + Y_4{}^{-4}) \qquad (2\text{-}27)$$

where $A_0{}^0 \propto Z/r_i$ and $A_4{}^0 \propto Z r^4/r_i{}^5$.

As is our usual practice, we assume solutions to our problem which can be expressed as a linear combination. In this case, we assume that the hydrogenlike d orbitals of the free ion are appropriate, with the only essential alteration being in the radial part of the wave function. Thus we write

$$\Psi = c_0 \psi_0 + c_{+1} \psi_{+1} + c_{-1} \psi_{-1} + c_{+2} \psi_{+2} + c_{-2} \psi_{-2}$$

where

$$\psi_0 = \frac{1}{4} \sqrt{\frac{5}{\pi}} R(r)(3 \cos^2 \theta - 1)$$

$$\psi_{\pm 1} = \frac{1}{2} \sqrt{\frac{15}{2\pi}} R(r)(\sin \theta \cos \theta) e^{\pm i\phi} \qquad (2\text{-}28)$$

$$\psi_{\pm 2} = \frac{1}{4} \sqrt{\frac{15}{2\pi}} R(r)(\sin^2 \theta) e^{\pm i 2\phi}$$

$R(r)$ is an appropriate radial function, and the angular dependence is included explicitly. The wave functions of Eqs. 2–28 are assumed to be exact solutions of a zeroth-order Hamiltonian with an appropriate effective nuclear charge, and we use them as a starting point for a perturbation calculation in which the perturbing interaction is V_c. Evaluation of the matrix elements of V_c using the functions of Eqs. 2–28 shows that the $A_0{}^0 Y_0{}^0$ term serves only to shift all of the energy levels equally. Splitting comes about through the remaining parts of the perturbation Hamiltonian. The matrix elements of these remaining terms are all of the form nDq, where n is an integer, D is a parameter involving the ligand distance, $35e/4r_i{}^5$, and q is a number which can in principle be determined by an integration over the electronic wave function. Although q is not ordinarily calculated, it is an important experimental parameter. q is proportional to $\int_0^\infty R(r) r^4 R(r) r^2 \, dr = \overline{r^4}$, and as such it serves as a very sensitive indication of the radial distribution function of an electron.

The complete secular determinant of the perturbation has the form,

$$\begin{vmatrix} (Dq - \bar{E}) & 0 & 0 & 0 & 5Dq \\ 0 & (-4Dq - \bar{E}) & 0 & 0 & 0 \\ 0 & 0 & (-6Dq - \bar{E}) & 0 & 0 \\ 0 & 0 & 0 & (-4Dq - \bar{E}) & 0 \\ 5Dq & 0 & 0 & 0 & (Dq - \bar{E}) \end{vmatrix} = 0$$

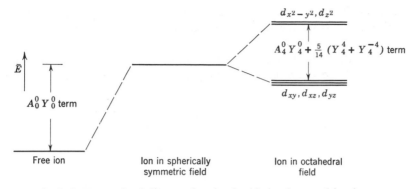

Fig. 2–5   Energy-level diagram for the d orbitals of a metal ion in an octahedral field.

the roots of which are

$$\bar{E}_1 = \bar{E}_2 = +6Dq$$
$$\bar{E}_3 = \bar{E}_4 = \bar{E}_5 = -4Dq$$

Evaluation of the c's by the usual procedure leads to the following wave functions:

$$\Psi_1 = \psi_0 \qquad\qquad (= d_{z^2})$$

$$\Psi_2 = \frac{1}{\sqrt{2}}(\psi_2 + \psi_{-2}) \qquad (= d_{x^2-y^2})$$

$$\Psi_3 = \frac{1}{\sqrt{2}}(\psi_1 + \psi_{-1}) \qquad (= d_{xz}) \tag{2–29}$$

$$\Psi_4 = \frac{-i}{\sqrt{2}}(\psi_1 - \psi_{-1}) \qquad (= d_{yz})$$

$$\Psi_5 = \frac{-i}{\sqrt{2}}(\psi_2 - \psi_{-2}) \qquad (= d_{xy})$$

The specification of these functions in terms of the indicated cartesian coordinates follows directly from the form of the functions of Eqs. 2–28, noting that $e^{i\phi} = \cos\phi + i\sin\phi$, and that $x \propto \sin\theta\cos\phi$, $y \propto \sin\theta\sin\phi$, and $z \propto \cos\theta$. The splittings are shown diagramatically in Fig. 2–5. We are generally concerned only with the splittings usually represented on an abbreviated diagram of the form shown in Fig. 2–6.

Note that some additional nomenclature is introduced here. Since $10Dq$ is a parameter which must be determined experimentally, it is customary to use the simpler symbol Δ to represent this crystal-field splitting. The e_g and t_{2g} classifications have their origin in group theory, and will be used simply as an alternative notation for our purposes. It will be observed that our splitting pattern follows a *center-of-gravity* rule, i.e., $\Delta_{e_g} = \frac{3}{5}\Delta$ and $\Delta_{t_{2g}} = -\frac{2}{5}\Delta$. This is a perfectly general result which follows from the fact that closed shells must be spherically symmetric.

Now that the real forms of the d orbitals have been derived, we could equally well use them as the starting point for a qualitative discussion

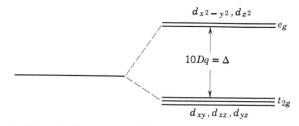

Fig. 2–6   Abbreviated energy-level diagram for the d orbitals of a metal ion in an octahedral field.

of splittings in various crystalline fields with which the reader is undoubtedly familiar. The orbitals are of the form shown in Fig. 2–7 and represent a set equally as good as the original orbitals, because any linear combination of solutions is also an acceptable solution of the zeroth-order wave equation.

The crystal-field-splitting parameter Δ is usually found experimentally to fall in the range

$$10{,}000 \text{ cm}^{-1} \leqslant \Delta \leqslant 30{,}000 \text{ cm}^{-1}$$

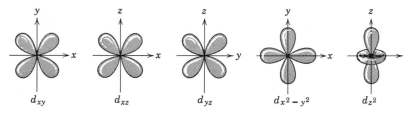

Fig. 2–7   Form of the real d orbitals of a metal ion.

for octahedral complexes. The exact value will depend on many factors, but as a general rule, it is found that Δ is strongly influenced by the nature of the ligands. This allows an ordering of ligands with respect to their *ligand-field strengths*. Such a sequence is known as the *Tsuchida*, or *spectrochemical series:*

$$\text{I}^- < \text{Br}^- < \text{Cl}^- < \text{F}^- < \text{C}_2\text{H}_5\text{OH} < \text{H}_2\text{O} < \text{NH}_3$$
$$< \text{H}_2\text{NCH}_2\text{CH}_2\text{NH}_2 < \text{NO}_2^- < \text{CN}^-$$

An often cited example of the result of these orbital splittings is the optical spectrum of the $\text{Ti}(\text{H}_2\text{O})_6^{3+}$ ion. The Ti^{3+} ion is in an essentially octahedral environment, with a d^1 configuration. A band which is very broad and of very small extinction is found at about 20,000 cm^{-1} and is assigned to the $t_{2g} \to e_g$ transition. The small extinction is attributed to the fact that the transition is forbidden by *LaPort's rule*. This is true of optical transitions of transition metal complexes in general, and is due to the fact that the matrix elements of the electric-dipole transition operator between pure d states all vanish. The fact that they do appear to a certain limited extent indicates that at least one of the assumptions made in the foregoing treatment is not completely valid. Actually, mixing with ligand orbitals as well as with p atomic orbitals of the metal atom seem to be important factors in this regard.

The broadness of the absorption band is attributed to two causes primarily. The first of these is vibronic coupling, i.e., the interaction of vibrational and electronic energies. The net effect is a broadening of the energy states into bands, the width of which can be reduced by lowering the temperature because then the vibrational activity is greatly suppressed. The second broadening factor is a small distortion due to the *Jahn-Teller effect*. Jahn and Teller proved many years ago that a molecule cannot exist in an orbitally degenerate ground state. A distortion of the configuration will occur in such a way as to remove this degeneracy. We cannot on the basis of the theory predict how the molecule will distort, or what the extent of the distortion will be. These distortions are generally of such a magnitude as to broaden the optical-absorption bands, actual Jahn-Teller splittings seldom being observed. We will consider some of these effects in more detail later.

2-4 ANGULAR MOMENTUM AND THE MAGNETIC PROPERTIES OF ELEMENTARY PARTICLES

In classical mechanics, angular momentum turns out to be a constant of the motion in the absence of external forces and, as such, it plays an extremely important role. In quantum mechanics, angular momentum enjoys a similar unique position. In this case, we describe it as being characterized by *good quantum numbers*.

Angular momentum is defined classically as

$$\mathbf{M} = \mathbf{r} \times m\mathbf{v} = \mathbf{r} \times \mathbf{p} \qquad (2\text{-}30)$$

where $\mathbf{r}$ is the radius vector and $\mathbf{p}$ is the momentum. By components,

$$M_x = yp_z - zp_y$$
$$M_y = zp_x - xp_z$$
$$M_z = xp_y - yp_x$$

and we can easily construct the following quantum-mechanical operators by using the rules previously discussed:

$$\hat{M}_x = -i\hbar\left(y\frac{\partial}{\partial z} - z\frac{\partial}{\partial y}\right)$$

$$\hat{M}_y = -i\hbar\left(z\frac{\partial}{\partial x} - x\frac{\partial}{\partial z}\right)$$

$$\hat{M}_z = -i\hbar\left(x\frac{\partial}{\partial y} - y\frac{\partial}{\partial x}\right)$$

$$\hat{M}^2 = \hat{M}_x{}^2 + \hat{M}_y{}^2 + \hat{M}_z{}^2$$

(2–31)

It can readily be shown that $\hat{M}_x$, $\hat{M}_y$, and $\hat{M}_z$ do not commute[1] but rather,

$$\hat{M}_x\hat{M}_y - \hat{M}_y\hat{M}_x = i\hbar\hat{M}_z$$

$$\hat{M}_y\hat{M}_z - \hat{M}_z\hat{M}_y = i\hbar\hat{M}_x$$

$$\hat{M}_z\hat{M}_x - \hat{M}_x\hat{M}_z = i\hbar\hat{M}_y$$

(2–32)

However, $\hat{M}^2$ and $\hat{M}_z$ do commute:

$$\hat{M}^2\hat{M}_z - \hat{M}_z\hat{M}^2 = 0$$

(2–33)

It can be shown that for a pair of commuting quantum-mechanical operators, there exists a set of eigenfunctions which are simultaneously eigenfunctions of both operators. In this case, it is the spherical harmonics which were previously defined (Sec. 2–3, p. 19). It is found that the only allowed eigenvalues are given by

$$\hat{M}^2 Y_l{}^m = l(l + 1)\hbar^2 Y_l{}^m$$

(2–34)

and

$$\hat{M}_z Y_l{}^m = m\hbar Y_l{}^m$$

(2–35)

with $-l \leq m \leq l$ in integral steps. This means that the angular momentum is quantized along the characteristic axis, and that the only observable values are $m\hbar$. The actual length of the angular-momentum vector is $\sqrt{l(l + 1)}\hbar$, so that the z-component can never be observed exactly along the axis of quantization.[2]

Since $\hat{M}_y$ and $\hat{M}_x$ do not commute with $\hat{M}_z$ or themselves, the spherical harmonics will not be eigenfunctions of these operators. They are nevertheless important operators, as we shall see, and it is convenient to define

---

[1] Two quantum-mechanical operators are said to commute if $\hat{X}\hat{Y} - \hat{Y}\hat{X} = 0$.
[2] Note that this would represent a violation of the uncertainty principle if it were possible.

raising and lowering operators by the combinations,

$$\hat{M}_+ = \hat{M}_x + i\hat{M}_y$$
$$\hat{M}_- = \hat{M}_x - i\hat{M}_y \qquad (2\text{--}36)$$

The choice of these names is obvious if we observe how they operate on the spherical harmonics:

$$\hat{M}_+ Y_l^m = \sqrt{l(l+1) - m(m+1)}\,\hbar Y_l^{m+1}$$
$$= \sqrt{(l-m)(l+m+1)}\,\hbar Y_l^{m+1}$$
$$\hat{M}_- Y_l^m = \sqrt{l(l+1) - m(m-1)}\,\hbar Y_l^{m-1} \qquad (2\text{--}37)$$
$$= \sqrt{(l+m)(l-m+1)}\,\hbar Y_l^{m-1}$$

A nonvanishing expectation value for the orbital angular momentum implies a component of motion about the center of mass. Since the moving particle under consideration here is an electron, this is tantamount to the consideration of a current flowing around a closed loop or ring, for which it can be shown that there is an associated magnetic moment,

$$\mu = \text{current} \times \text{area of ring}$$

With the current in electrostatic units (esu) and the magnetic moment in electromagnetic units (emu), we have

$$\mu = I \times \frac{\pi a^2}{c}$$

where c is the velocity of light. If the linear velocity is v, the frequency of revolution is $v/2\pi a$, so the current is given by

$$I = \frac{ev}{2\pi a}$$

and

$$\mu = \frac{eva}{2c}$$

The angular momentum, mva, we have found to be

$$mva = \sqrt{l(l+1)}\,\hbar$$

Thus,

$$\mu = \sqrt{l(l+1)}\,\frac{e\hbar}{2mc} = \sqrt{l(l+1)}\,\beta_M \qquad (2\text{--}38)$$

where

$$\beta_M = \frac{e\hbar}{2mc} \qquad (2\text{--}39)$$

is known as the *Bohr magneton*. Its numerical value is -9.27×10^{-21} erg/gauss.

It will be noted that the axis of the magnetic dipole is antiparallel to the angular-momentum vector because of the negative charge on the electron, and we write,

$$\mu = \frac{e}{2mc}\, \mathbf{M} \qquad (2\text{-}40)$$

If the characteristic z-axis is chosen at an angle θ with respect to the angular-momentum vector (see Fig. 2–8), then

$$\theta = \cos^{-1}\frac{m}{\sqrt{l(l+1)}}$$

and the component of the magnetic moment in any chosen direction must be

$$\mu \cos \theta = m\beta_M$$

The above relationships have taken only the orbital motion of electrons into consideration. In 1925, Goudsmit and Uhlenbeck postulated the existence of an *intrinsic angular momentum*, or *spin*, to explain fine struc-

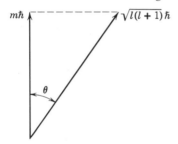

ture effects in atomic spectra. In this case, the l quantum number is limited to a value of $\frac{1}{2}$, so that $m = \pm\frac{1}{2}$. All of the above results are applicable, except that the proportionality factor relating spin and its associated magnetic moment is *twice as large* as that of orbital motion:

$$\mu = \frac{e}{mc}\, \mathbf{S} \qquad (2\text{-}41)$$

Fig. 2–8 Projection of the angular-momentum vector along a given axis.

The total magnetic moment associated with the electron obviously depends on the exact manner in which the spin and orbital magnetic moments couple together. With $\mathbf{J}$ defined as the total angular momentum (in units of $\hbar$), we write

$$\mu = g\frac{e\hbar}{2mc}\, \mathbf{J} = g\beta_M\mathbf{J} = \gamma\hbar\mathbf{J} \qquad (2\text{-}42)$$

γ, the ratio of magnetic moment to angular momentum, is known as the *magnetogyric ratio* (sometimes called *gyromagnetic ratio*); g is called the spectroscopic splitting factor, the Landé g factor, or simply the g factor. It is

$$g = 1 + \frac{J(J+1) + S(S+1) - L(L+1)}{2J(J+1)} \qquad (2\text{-}43)$$

for the usual Russell-Saunders coupling, which for the case of pure spin-only angular momentum ($L = 0$) takes on the value 2. More exact calculations with electrodynamic effects included give a value of 2.00229 for the free-spin g value.

By arguments analogous to the foregoing, we write for a nucleus of spin $\mathbf{I}$,

$$\boldsymbol{\mu} = \gamma_N \hbar \mathbf{I} = g_N \beta_N \mathbf{I} \qquad (2\text{-}44)$$

where γ_N is the *nuclear magnetogyric ratio*, g_N is the *nuclear g factor*, and β_N is the *nuclear magneton*. The nuclear magneton is defined in terms of the proton mass,

$$\beta_N = \frac{e\hbar}{2M_p c}$$

and is numerically 5.05×10^{-24} erg/gauss.

The concept of nuclear spin is not new. It actually predated that of the electron spin, having been suggested in 1924 by Pauli. We do not understand nuclear interactions sufficiently well at the present time to be able to compound the properties for individual nucleons to derive those for a composite nucleus, however. Both positive and negative moments are possible, the latter case resulting from a predominance of the effect of the neutrons.[1] Notwithstanding these difficulties, certain systematics which are very useful can be observed by studying the charts of the nuclides. It is found that:

1. If the mass number A is odd, the nuclear spin is half-integral.
2. If the mass number A and the charge number Z are both even, the spin is zero.
3. If the mass number A is even but the charge number Z is odd, the spin is integral.

Naturally, only those nuclei with a spin and an associated magnetic moment will be of interest to us. Table 2-1 lists the stable isotopes and their moments.

2-5 ELECTRIC-QUADRUPOLE MOMENTS

Another nuclear property which is of some importance in magnetic resonance work is the *electric-quadrupole moment*. It is related to the spin, and is a measure of the deviation from a spherical charge distribution within the nucleus. It is found that only nuclei with spins greater than $\frac{1}{2}$ possess electric-quadrupole moments.

---

[1] The neutron itself has a negative magnetic moment, and can be thought of as having a negative charge at a larger average distance from the center than that of the positive charge (which is of course equal in magnitude).

Table 2–1   *Magnetic Moments**

Isotope	Abundance, %	Magnetic Moment†	Spin	Electric-Quadrupole Moment‡
Free electron	—	−1836	$\frac{1}{2}$	—
H^1	99.9844	2.79268	$\frac{1}{2}$	—
H^2	1.56×10^{-2}	0.85738	1	2.77×10^{-3}
He^3	$\sim 10^{-6}$	−2.1274	$\frac{1}{2}$	—
Li^6	7.43	0.82192	1	4.6×10^{-4}
Li^7	92.57	3.2560	$\frac{3}{2}$	−0.1
Be^9	100.	−1.1773	$\frac{3}{2}$	2×10^{-2}
B^{10}	18.83	1.8005	3	7.4×10^{-2}
B^{11}	81.17	2.6880	$\frac{3}{2}$	3.55×10^{-2}
C^{13}	1.108	0.70220	$\frac{1}{2}$	—
N^{14}	99.635	0.40358	1	7.1×10^{-2}
N^{15}	0.365	−0.28304	$\frac{1}{2}$	—
O^{17}	3.7×10^{-2}	−1.8930	$\frac{5}{2}$	-4×10^{-3}
F^{19}	100.	2.6273	$\frac{1}{2}$	—
Ne^{21}	0.257	−0.66176	$\frac{3}{2}$	—
Na^{23}	100.	2.2161	$\frac{3}{2}$	0.1
Mg^{25}	10.05	−0.85471	$\frac{5}{2}$	—
Al^{27}	100.	3.6385	$\frac{5}{2}$	0.149
Si^{29}	4.70	−0.55477	$\frac{1}{2}$	—
P^{31}	100.	1.1305	$\frac{1}{2}$	—
S^{33}	0.74	0.64274	$\frac{3}{2}$	−0.053
Cl^{35}	75.4	0.82091	$\frac{3}{2}$	-7.9×10^{-2}
Cl^{37}	24.6	0.68330	$\frac{3}{2}$	-6.21×10^{-2}
K^{39}	93.08	0.39094	$\frac{3}{2}$	−0.07
K^{41}	6.91	0.21488	$\frac{3}{2}$	—
Ca^{43}	0.13	−1.3153	$\frac{7}{2}$	—
Sc^{45}	100.	4.7492	$\frac{7}{2}$	−0.22
Ti^{47}	7.75	−0.78711	$\frac{5}{2}$	—
Ti^{49}	5.51	−1.1022	$\frac{7}{2}$	—
V^{50}	0.24	3.3413	6	—
V^{51}	$\sim 100.$	5.1392	$\frac{7}{2}$	0.2
Cr^{53}	9.54	−0.47354	$\frac{3}{2}$	—
Mn^{55}	100.	3.4611	$\frac{5}{2}$	0.6
Fe^{57}	2.245	0.0903	$\frac{1}{2}$	—
Co^{59}	100.	4.6388	$\frac{7}{2}$	0.5
Ni^{61}	1.25	0.746	$\frac{3}{2}$	—
Cu^{63}	69.09	2.2206	$\frac{3}{2}$	−0.16
Cu^{65}	30.91	2.3790	$\frac{3}{2}$	−0.15
Zn^{67}	4.12	0.87354	$\frac{5}{2}$	0.18
Ga^{69}	60.2	2.0108	$\frac{3}{2}$	0.178
Ga^{71}	39.8	2.5549	$\frac{3}{2}$	0.112

Table 2–1 (Continued)

Isotope	Abundance, %	Magnetic Moment†	Spin	Electric-Quadrupole Moment‡
Ge^{73}	7.61	−0.87677	$\frac{9}{2}$	−0.2
As^{75}	100.	1.4349	$\frac{3}{2}$	0.3
Se^{77}	7.50	0.5325	$\frac{1}{2}$	—
Br^{79}	50.57	2.0991	$\frac{3}{2}$	0.34
Br^{81}	49.43	2.2626	$\frac{3}{2}$	0.28
Kr^{83}	11.55	−0.96705	$\frac{9}{2}$	0.15
Rb^{85}	72.8	1.3482	$\frac{5}{2}$	0.28
Rb^{87}	27.2	2.7414	$\frac{3}{2}$	0.14
Sr^{87}	7.02	−1.0893	$\frac{9}{2}$	—
Y^{89}	100.	−0.13682	$\frac{1}{2}$	—
Zr^{91}	11.23	−1.298	$\frac{5}{2}$	—
Nb^{93}	100.	6.1435	$\frac{9}{2}$	−0.16
Mo^{95}	15.78	−0.9099	$\frac{5}{2}$	—
Mo^{97}	9.60	−0.9290	$\frac{5}{2}$	—
Ru^{99}	12.81	0.63	$\frac{5}{2}$	—
Ru^{101}	16.98	−0.69	$\frac{5}{2}$	—
Rh^{103}	100.	−0.0879	$\frac{1}{2}$	—
Pd^{105}	22.23	−0.57	$\frac{5}{2}$	—
Ag^{107}	51.35	−0.1130	$\frac{1}{2}$	—
Ag^{109}	48.65	−0.1299	$\frac{1}{2}$	—
Cd^{111}	12.86	−0.5922	$\frac{1}{2}$	—
Cd^{113}	12.34	−0.6195	$\frac{1}{2}$	—
In^{113}	4.16	5.4960	$\frac{9}{2}$	0.750
Sn^{115}	0.35	−0.9132	$\frac{1}{2}$	—
Sn^{117}	7.67	−0.9949	$\frac{1}{2}$	—
Sn^{119}	8.68	−1.0409	$\frac{1}{2}$	—
Sb^{121}	57.25	3.3417	$\frac{5}{2}$	0.53
Sb^{123}	42.75	2.5334	$\frac{7}{2}$	0.68
Te^{123}	0.89	−0.7319	$\frac{1}{2}$	—
Te^{125}	7.03	−0.8824	$\frac{1}{2}$	—
I^{127}	100.	2.7937	$\frac{5}{2}$	−0.75
Xe^{129}	26.24	−0.77255	$\frac{1}{2}$	—
Xe^{131}	21.24	0.68680	$\frac{3}{2}$	−0.12
Cs^{133}	100.	2.5642	$\frac{7}{2}$	0.004
Ba^{135}	6.59	0.83229	$\frac{3}{2}$	—
Ba^{137}	11.32	0.93107	$\frac{3}{2}$	—
La^{139}	99.911	2.7615	$\frac{7}{2}$	0.5
Pr^{141}	100.	3.92	$\frac{5}{2}$	-5.4×10^{-2}
Nd^{143}	12.20	−1.25	$\frac{7}{2}$	−0.57
Nd^{145}	8.30	−0.78	$\frac{7}{2}$	−0.30
Sm^{147}	15.07	−0.68	$\frac{7}{2}$	0.72

Table 2–1   (Continued)

Isotope	Abundance, %	Magnetic Moment†	Spin	Electric-Quadrupole Moment‡
Sm^{149}	13.84	−0.55	$\frac{7}{2}$	0.72
Eu^{151}	47.77	3.441	$\frac{5}{2}$	—
Eu^{153}	52.23	1.521	$\frac{5}{2}$	—
Eu^{154}	—	2.0	3	—
Gd^{155}	14.68	−0.25	$\frac{3}{2}$	1.1
Gd^{157}	15.64	−0.34	$\frac{3}{2}$	1.0
Tb^{159}	100.	1.52	$\frac{3}{2}$	—
Dy^{161}	18.73	−0.38	$\frac{5}{2}$	—
Dy^{163}	24.97	−0.53	$\frac{5}{2}$	—
Ho^{165}	100.	3.31	$\frac{7}{2}$	2
Er^{167}	22.82	0.48	$\frac{7}{2}$	(10)
Tm^{169}	100.	−0.20	$\frac{1}{2}$	—
Yb^{171}	14.27	0.4926	$\frac{1}{2}$	—
Yb^{173}	16.08	−0.677	$\frac{5}{2}$	—
Lu^{175}	97.40	2.9	$\frac{7}{2}$	5.5
Hf^{177}	18.39	0.61	$\frac{7}{2}$	3
Hf^{179}	13.78	−0.47	$\frac{9}{2}$	3
Ta^{181}	100.	2.340	$\frac{7}{2}$	4.0
W^{183}	14.28	0.115	$\frac{1}{2}$	—
Re^{185}	37.07	3.1437	$\frac{5}{2}$	2.8
Re^{187}	62.93	3.1760	$\frac{5}{2}$	2.6
Os^{187}	—	0.12	$\frac{1}{2}$	—
Os^{189}	16.1	0.6507	$\frac{3}{2}$	2.0
Ir^{191}	38.5	0.16	$\frac{3}{2}$	1.5
Ir^{193}	61.5	0.17	$\frac{3}{2}$	1.5
Pt^{195}	33.7	0.6004	$\frac{1}{2}$	—
Au^{197}	100.	0.1439	$\frac{3}{2}$	0.56
Hg^{199}	16.86	0.4979	$\frac{1}{2}$	—
Hg^{201}	13.24	−0.5513	$\frac{3}{2}$	0.45
Tl^{203}	29.52	1.5960	$\frac{1}{2}$	—
Tl^{205}	70.48	1.6115	$\frac{1}{2}$	—
Pb^{207}	21.11	0.5837	$\frac{1}{2}$	—
Bi^{209}	100.	4.0389	$\frac{9}{2}$	−0.4

* Taken from a chart prepared by Varian Associates.
† In units of the nuclear magneton $e\hbar/2M_p c$.
‡ In units of $e \times 10^{-24}$ cm².

The nucleus can be regarded as a small, localized distribution of electric charge. If this is subjected to an electrostatic potential which originates from charges external to the localized distribution, the energy of interaction is given by

$$E = \int_v \rho V \, dv \qquad (2\text{–}45)$$

where ρ is the charge density, V is the electrostatic potential, and the integral is over the volume containing the localized distribution. Now let us expand the potential $V(x, y, z)$ in a Taylor's series about an origin situated at the center of charge. In tensor notation,[1] this is

$$V(x, y, z) = V_0 + \frac{\partial V}{\partial x_j}\bigg|_0 x_j + \frac{1}{2\,!} \frac{\partial^2 V}{\partial x_j \, \partial x_k}\bigg|_0 x_j x_k + \cdots$$

Each of the derivatives appearing in this expression is evaluated at the origin of coordinates, and is a constant. Using this expansion, we obtain for the energy,

$$E = V_0 \int_v \rho \, dv + \frac{\partial V}{\partial x_j}\bigg|_0 \int_v \rho x_j \, dv + \frac{1}{2\,!} \frac{\partial^2 V}{\partial x_j \, \partial x_k}\bigg|_0 \int_v \rho x_j x_k \, dv + \cdots \qquad (2\text{–}46)$$

The integrals which appear in this equation are called the *moments* of the distribution, and are actually tensor quantities of various ranks. The first integral

$$\int_v \rho \, dv = Q \qquad (2\text{–}47)$$

is just the *net charge* (electric monopole), which is a scalar quantity or a zero-rank tensor. There are three integrals in the second term of the type

$$\int_v \rho x_j \, dv = p_j \qquad (2\text{–}48)$$

They are the components of a vector representing the electric-dipole moment, and make up a first-rank tensor. The nine integrals of the third term,

$$\int_v \rho x_j x_k \, dv = Q_{jk} \qquad (2\text{–}49)$$

are the components of a 3×3 matrix representing the electric-quadrupole moment of the distribution, which is a second-rank tensor. In general, it is not necessary to consider higher moments, although this analysis can readily be extended to higher-order terms if necessary.

To this degree of approximation, the energy of interaction in terms of

[1] This simply means that $x_i, x_j, x_k \equiv x, y, z$, and that the recurrence of a subscript in a given term implies summation over that subscript.

these moments is

$$E = QV_0 + p_j \frac{\partial V}{\partial x_j}\bigg|_0 + \tfrac{1}{2} Q_{jk} \frac{\partial^2 V}{\partial x_j \, \partial x_k}\bigg|_0 \qquad (2\text{--}50)$$

The first two terms of this expression are readily identified. The first is the net charge times the potential at the origin, and the second is the scalar product of the electric-dipole moment with the potential gradient. The latter term is the orientation energy of an electric dipole in an electric field, and in more familiar notation is

$$p_j \frac{\partial V}{\partial x_j}\bigg|_0 = -\mathbf{p} \cdot (-\nabla V|_0) = -\mathbf{p} \cdot \mathbf{E}_0 \qquad (2\text{--}51)$$

The quadrupole term can be thought of as various components of Q_{jk} being "acted upon" by corresponding electric-field-gradient components. Since these gradients vanish for uniform fields, an electric-quadrupole

Fig. 2–9   Nuclear charge distributions.

interaction exists only if there is an *inhomogeneous field* at the nuclear position.

We will usually be concerned with those cases for which the charge distribution is cylindrically symmetric about a particular axis, which is chosen as the z-axis. In this case the quadrupole tensor is diagonal,

$$\mathbf{Q} = \begin{pmatrix} Q_{xx} & 0 & 0 \\ 0 & Q_{yy} & 0 \\ 0 & 0 & Q_{zz} \end{pmatrix} = \begin{pmatrix} \int \rho x^2 \, dv & 0 & 0 \\ 0 & \int \rho y^2 \, dv & 0 \\ 0 & 0 & \int \rho z^2 \, dv \end{pmatrix}$$

$$(2\text{--}52)$$

and the quadrupole-interaction energy is given by

$$E_Q = \tfrac{1}{2} Q_{xx} \frac{\partial^2 V}{\partial x^2} + \tfrac{1}{2} Q_{yy} \frac{\partial^2 V}{\partial y^2} + \tfrac{1}{2} Q_{zz} \frac{\partial^2 V}{\partial z^2} \qquad (2\text{--}53)$$

Because of the cylindrical symmetry, $Q_{xx} = Q_{yy}$, and because the electrostatic potential arises from external charges, it must satisfy Laplace's equation (Eq. 2–25). Thus,

$$\frac{\partial^2 V}{\partial x^2} + \frac{\partial^2 V}{\partial y^2} + \frac{\partial^2 V}{\partial z^2} = 0$$

and the interaction energy is

$$E_Q = \tfrac{1}{2}(Q_{zz} - Q_{xx})\frac{\partial^2 V}{\partial z^2} \tag{2-54}$$

We generally write this in terms of a single quantity Q in units of e:

$$E_Q = \tfrac{1}{4}eQ\frac{\partial^2 V}{\partial z^2} \tag{2-55}$$

We can readily show that $Q = 0$ for a spherically symmetric charge distribution, $Q > 0$ for a prolate, $Q < 0$ for an oblate spheroidal distribution (see Fig. 2–9).

SUPPLEMENTARY READING

1. C. A. Coulson, *Valence*, Oxford University Press, New York, 2nd Edition, 1961.
2. Y. K. Syrkin, and M. E. Dyatkina, *Structure of Molecules and the Chemical Bond*, Dover Publications, New York, 1964.
3. J. W. Linnett, *Wave Mechanics and Valency*, John Wiley & Sons, New York, 1960.
4. L. E. Orgel, *An Introduction to Transition-Metal Chemistry*, John Wiley & Sons, New York, 1960.
5. R. B. Leighton, *Principles of Modern Physics*, McGraw-Hill Book Company, New York, 1959.
6. W. Kauzmann, *Quantum Chemistry*, Academic Press, New York, 1957.
7. C. J. Ballhausen, and H. B. Gray, *Molecular Orbital Theory*, W. A. Benjamin, New York, 1964.
8. B. N. Figgis, *Introduction to Ligand Fields*, John Wiley & Sons, New York, 1966.

3

Basic Magnetic Resonance Theory

3–1 EFFECTS OF STATIC MAGNETIC FIELDS

When an atom or a molecule is placed in a magnetic field, there is an alignment of the magnetic moments associated with the electrons as well as the nuclei, and an effect known as *static paramagnetism* is observed. In addition, orbital motions are induced which endow all materials with a certain amount of diamagnetism. These effects influence the macroscopic properties and also the microscopic properties which are observed by magnetic resonance spectroscopy. Thus, a consideration of some aspects of the theory of magnetic susceptibilities is in order before we proceed with the resonance theory.

We begin by defining several terms with which we must become familiar. The *magnetic induction* $\mathbf{B}$ and the *magnetic field* $\mathbf{H}$ are related by (in emu)[1]

$$\mathbf{B} = \mathbf{H} + 4\pi\mathbf{M} \qquad (3\text{–}1)$$

where $\mathbf{M}$ is known as the *magnetization* and represents the magnetic moment per unit volume. With the exception of the highly ordered ferromagnetic and antiferromagnetic materials, it is found that the magnetization is proportional to the magnetic field in isotropic media:

$$\mathbf{M} = \chi_v\mathbf{H} \qquad (3\text{–}2)$$

The proportionality constant χ_v is known as the *volume magnetic susceptibility*. A substance for which $\chi_v > 0$ is called *paramagnetic*, and if $\chi_v < 0$ it is called *diamagnetic*. With both $\mathbf{M}$ and $\mathbf{H}$ expressed in magnetic-field units, χ_v is obviously a dimensionless quantity. It ranges from about -10^{-6} for most common materials to values of opposite sign and several orders of magnitude larger for materials which contain unpaired electrons. As we shall soon see, susceptibilities of paramagnetic materials have an

---

[1] Chemists almost without exception use H when they really mean B. After pointing out this error in usage, we will bow to tradition and write all of our subsequent equations with H, but the distinction should be kept in mind.

inverse temperature dependence, whereas the susceptibility for diamagnetic materials is largely independent of temperature. Magnetic-susceptibility data can alternatively be expressed in terms of the *magnetic susceptibility per gram*, χ, and the *molar magnetic susceptibility*, χ_M, which are related by

$$\chi_M = M\chi = \frac{M\chi_v}{d} \tag{3-3}$$

where M is the molecular weight and d is the density.

Diamagnetic Susceptibility

Let us first consider the behavior of an atom in a magnetic field. Each electron in a given atom will be subjected to two forces: the first is due to the interaction with the magnetic field,

$$\mathbf{F}_H = -\frac{e}{c}(\mathbf{v} \times \mathbf{H})$$

and the second is due to the interaction with the electric field of the nucleus:

$$\mathbf{F}_E = -e\mathbf{E}$$

Using Newton's laws, the equation of motion is written as

$$m\frac{d^2\mathbf{r}}{dt^2} = -\frac{e}{c}\left(\frac{d\mathbf{r}}{dt} \times \mathbf{H}\right) - e\mathbf{E} \tag{3-4}$$

This equation is most readily solved by consideration of the behavior of a vector in a rotating coordinate system. The change in the radius vector $\mathbf{r}$ in a time dt in the *body-fixed axes* differs from the corresponding change in the *space-fixed axes* only by the effect of the rotation of the body axes:

$$(d\mathbf{r})_b = (d\mathbf{r})_s + (d\mathbf{r})_{\text{rot}} \tag{3-5}$$

The rotation vector $\boldsymbol{\Omega}$ is defined in such a way that for an infinitesimal rotation, $d\mathbf{r} = \mathbf{r} \times d\boldsymbol{\Omega}$, as can be seen in Fig. 3-1. With the angular velocity given by $\boldsymbol{\omega} = d\boldsymbol{\Omega}/dt$, the following equation follows immediately for the time rate of change of $\mathbf{r}$:

$$\left(\frac{d\mathbf{r}}{dt}\right)_s = \left(\frac{d\mathbf{r}}{dt}\right)_b + \boldsymbol{\omega} \times \mathbf{r} \tag{3-6}$$

or

$$\mathbf{v}_s = \mathbf{v}_b + \boldsymbol{\omega} \times \mathbf{r} \tag{3-7}$$

Differentiation of Eq. 3–7 gives, using an equation analogous to Eq. 3–6 for **v**,

$$\frac{d\mathbf{v}_s}{dt} = \mathbf{a}_s = \left(\frac{d\mathbf{v}_s}{dt}\right)_b + \boldsymbol{\omega} \times \mathbf{v}_s$$

$$= \left[\frac{d}{dt}(\mathbf{v}_b + \boldsymbol{\omega} \times \mathbf{r})\right]_b + \boldsymbol{\omega} \times (\mathbf{v}_b + \boldsymbol{\omega} \times \mathbf{r})$$

$$= \left(\frac{d\mathbf{v}_b}{dt}\right)_b + \left(\frac{d\boldsymbol{\omega}}{dt} \times \mathbf{r}\right)_b + \left(\boldsymbol{\omega} \times \frac{d\mathbf{r}}{dt}\right)_b + \boldsymbol{\omega} \times \mathbf{v}_b + \boldsymbol{\omega} \times (\boldsymbol{\omega} \times \mathbf{r})$$

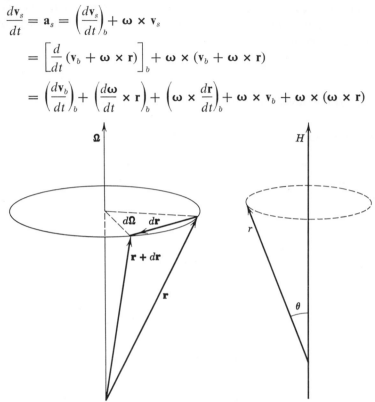

Fig. 3–1   Change in a vector produced by an infinitesimal rotation.

Fig. 3–2   Coordinates for the rotation of electrons about the applied magnetic-field direction.

If **ω** is constant,

$$\mathbf{a}_s = \mathbf{a}_b + 2\boldsymbol{\omega} \times \mathbf{v}_b + \boldsymbol{\omega} \times (\boldsymbol{\omega} \times \mathbf{r}) \tag{3–8}$$

Using Eq. 3–8, we can easily write the equation of motion for an electron, relative to a system of coordinates which is rotating at a constant angular velocity **ω**. In the *absence* of a magnetic field, it is

$$m\left[\frac{d^2\mathbf{r}}{dt^2} + 2\left(\boldsymbol{\omega} \times \frac{d\mathbf{r}}{dt}\right) + \boldsymbol{\omega} \times (\boldsymbol{\omega} \times \mathbf{r})\right] = -e\mathbf{E} \tag{3–9}$$

A comparison of Eq. 3–9 with Eq. 3–4 shows that the term

$$\frac{e}{c}\frac{d\mathbf{r}}{dt} \times \mathbf{H}$$

can be identified with $2m(\omega \times d\mathbf{r}/dt) + m\omega \times (\omega \times \mathbf{r})$. If $\mathbf{H}$ is not too large, ω must be small, and terms of order ω^2 can be neglected. Then, the two equations become identical if

$$\omega = -\frac{e}{2mc}\mathbf{H} \tag{3-10}$$

Thus we conclude that the magnetic field produces a rotation of the electron about the field direction, with the angular velocity being proportional to the magnetic-field strength as given by Eq. 3–10. This is known as *Larmor precession*.

Associated with this induced electron rotation is a magnetic moment. The magnitude of this moment can be calculated as follows: Assume the electron to be at a distance r from the center of the atom, and suppose that the radius vector is at an angle θ with respect to the magnetic-field direction (Fig. 3–2). The current is given by

$$e\frac{\omega}{2\pi} = -\frac{e^2H}{4\pi mc}$$

Since the area swept out by this motion is $\pi(r \sin \theta)^2$, the magnetic moment is (see Sec. 2–4),

$$\mu = -\frac{e^2H}{4mc^2}r^2 \sin^2 \theta$$

The negative sign, of course, means that the moment is opposed to the direction of the applied field (a diamagnetic effect). This result is not satisfactory as it stands in terms of our wave-mechanical picture of the atom, for which we cannot have well-defined values of r. This difficulty can be removed by replacing r^2 by its quantum-mechanical expectation value,

$$\overline{r^2} = \int_0^\infty R(r)r^2R(r)r^2 \, dr$$

where $R(r)$ is the appropriate radial distribution function for the electron. Furthermore, since the atom is spherically symmetric, we replace $\sin^2 \theta$ by its average value $\frac{2}{3}$. Thus, the magnetic moment per atom is

$$\mu = -\frac{e^2H}{6mc^2}\sum_i \overline{r_i^2}$$

where the sum is taken over all electrons in the atom. Finally, the molar diamagnetic susceptibility is given by

$$\chi_M = -\frac{Ne^2}{6mc^2}\sum_i \overline{r_i^2} \tag{3-11}$$

In this equation, N is Avogadro's number. This is, of course, just the induced susceptibility, and takes no account of an intrinsic moment due to spin or normal orbital motion.

The extension of the foregoing treatment to molecules is complicated by several factors, not the least of which is the fact that induced electronic currents depend on the orientation of the applied magnetic field with respect to the fixed nuclear framework. As a result, the magnetic moment, and hence the magnetization, may no longer be parallel to $\mathbf{H}$. This implies that the susceptibility is not a scalar quantity in this case, but must be represented by a second-rank tensor. In liquids and gases where rapid reorientation of the molecules takes place, we naturally observe only the isotropic part. This is given by $\frac{1}{3}(\chi_1 + \chi_2 + \chi_3)$, where χ_1, χ_2, χ_3 are the principal values of the susceptibility tensor.

A very well-known example of the foregoing anisotropy of the susceptibility occurs in aromatic molecules. Here the anisotropy is very large, depending on whether the magnetic field is oriented in the plane or perpendicular to the plane of the molecule. It is thought that, in the latter case, ring currents can readily be induced in the π-electron cloud. Pauling has made calculations based upon this concept, applying the Larmor-frequency condition to electrons which are constrained to move about in such circular paths. The calculated values of the anisotropy are sufficiently close to those observed experimentally to contribute considerable confidence to the gross features of this model.

A second difficulty which restricts the foregoing arguments when applied to molecules is the fact that the electric field $\mathbf{E}$ is no longer spherically symmetric, so the equations of motion are different in the rotating and fixed reference frames. Only for a linear molecule in a cylindrically symmetric electronic state (a Σ state) is an analysis such as the aforementioned applicable. We obtain in this case,

$$\chi_M^{(z)} = -\frac{Ne^2}{4mc^2} \sum_i \overline{x_i^2 + y_i^2} \qquad (3\text{--}12)$$

Configuration interaction tends to mix excited states with the ground-state wave function, so that this result is not strictly valid. These excited states will, in general, be of lower symmetry; therefore the net effect is to hinder the free rotation of the charge cloud about the symmetry axis and thus reduce the diamagnetic susceptibility. Quantitative calculations by Van Vleck show that $\chi_M^{(z)}$ should actually be a sum of diamagnetic and paramagnetic terms of the form,

$$\chi_M^{(z)} = -\frac{Ne^2}{4mc^2} \sum_i \overline{x_i^2 + y_i^2} + \frac{Ne^2}{2m^2c^2} \sum_{n \neq 0} \frac{|\langle \psi_0| \hat{M}_z |\psi_n\rangle|^2}{E_n - E_0} \qquad (3\text{--}13)$$

where ψ_0 is the ground-state wave function, and the excited states are represented by ψ_n. The latter term is obviously positive, and if there happen to be low-lying excited states, it is possible to observe a weak paramagnetism in the absence of permanent electronic moments. Actual quantitative calculations with Eq. 3–13 are possible only in the simplest of cases. The difficulty is due to our limited knowledge of the excited states. Since $\chi_M^{(z)}$ is the sum of a negative (diamagnetic) term and a positive (paramagnetic) term, which are in some cases nearly equal in magnitude, quantitative calculations are quite meaningless for complex molecules. This same inherent difficulty will be encountered later when nuclear magnetic resonance (NMR) parameters are discussed.

Although *a priori* calculations of magnetic susceptibilities are not feasible, their experimental determination presents no difficulties, and there are compilations of them available in numerous places. As we shall presently see, the accurate determination of NMR parameters in some cases requires that they be known, and the values for some common materials are listed in Table 3–1. For substances whose diamagnetic susceptibilities are unknown, we can estimate them quite well by using a set of additive atomic contributions if constitutive corrections are also included. Such additive terms are known as *Pascal constants*, and a table of them can be found on page 19 of Ref. 3.[1] In mixtures, it is found that the molar susceptibilities are additive,

$$\chi_M \text{ (mixture)} = x_1 \chi_M(1) + x_2 \chi_M(2) \tag{3–14}$$

where x_1 and x_2 are the respective mole fractions. Similarly, if the molar volumes are additive, then

$$\chi_v \text{ (mixture)} = V_1 \chi_v(1) + V_2 \chi_v(2) \tag{3–15}$$

where V_1 and V_2 are the volume fractions of the respective components.

Paramagnetic Susceptibility

As noted in the foregoing, paramagnetism is observed in atoms, ions, and molecules in which there are permanent, resultant magnetic moments. Let us begin by considering the paramagnetism associated with the electronic moments.

By analogy with Eq. 2–51 the energy of interaction of a magnetic dipole in a magnetic field is given by

$$E = -\mu \cdot \mathbf{H} \tag{3–16}$$

[1] References are listed at the end of each chapter.

Table 3–1   *Volume Magnetic Susceptibilities of Some Common Materials*

Compound	Temperature, °C	$-\chi_v \times 10^6$, cgs units
Acetic acid	32	0.551
Acetone	20	0.460
Benzaldehyde	15	0.602
Benzene	32	0.611
Benzyl alcohol	15	0.697
Benzyl chloride	18	0.713
n-butyl alcohol	20	0.618
t-butyl alcohol	20	0.611
n-butyraldehyde	20	0.522
Carbon disulfide	20	0.68
Carbon tetrachloride	20	0.691
Cyclohexane	20	0.627
Ethyl acetate	20	0.554
Ethyl alcohol	20	0.575
Ethyl ether	20	0.534
Formamide	20	0.551
Glycerol	20	0.779
n-hexane	27	0.565
Isobutyl alcohol	20	0.624
Methyl alcohol	20	0.530
Methylene chloride	20	0.733
Nitric acid	22	0.467
n-propyl alcohol	20	0.605
Pyridine	20	0.611
Sulfuric acid	22	0.441
Toluene	20	0.618
Water	20	0.720
o-xylene	20	0.644
m-xylene	20	0.624
p-xylene	20	0.623

We have seen (see Eq. 2–42) that $\boldsymbol{\mu} = g\beta_M\mathbf{J}$, so that with $\mathbf{H}$ taken along the z-axis,

$$E = -g\beta_M H J_z$$

where $H = |\mathbf{H}|$. We are also well acquainted with the fact that J_z is restricted to values ranging from $-J$ to $+J$ in integral steps, and we can write,

$$E = g\beta_M H m \qquad (m = -J, -J + 1, \ldots, J - 1, J) \qquad (3\text{-}17)$$

We have defined the magnetization as the total magnetic moment per unit volume, and we need to evaluate it to calculate the susceptibility.

In terms of this definition, we can write,

$$\mathbf{M} = \frac{1}{V} \sum_i \mu_i$$

or, as the component along the axis of quantization,

$$M_z = \frac{1}{V} \sum_i \mu_{zi}$$

This can obviously be written in the form

$$M_z = N\bar{\mu}_z \qquad (3\text{--}18)$$

if $\bar{\mu}_z$ is defined as the average value of the individual moments, and N is the number of them per unit volume.

The average value of μ_z is

$$\bar{\mu}_z = \sum_j \mu_{zj} p_j$$

where the summation in this case is over the available quantized values of μ_z, and p_j is the probability that the magnetic moment has the value μ_{zj}. The probability is, of course, determined by the energy of the dipole in the magnetic field, which by the well-known Boltzmann equation is

$$p_j = \frac{e^{-E_j/kT}}{\sum_j e^{-E_j/kT}} = \frac{e^{g\beta_M H m_j/kT}}{\sum_{m_j=-J}^{+J} e^{g\beta_M H m_j/kT}} \qquad (3\text{--}19)$$

We find that

$$M_z = \frac{N \sum_{m_j=-J}^{+J} g\beta_M m_j e^{g\beta_M H m_j/kT}}{\sum_{m_j=-J}^{+J} e^{g\beta_M H m_j/kT}} \qquad (3\text{--}20)$$

This can be written as

$$M_z = Ng\beta_M J B_J(x) \qquad (3\text{--}21)$$

where $x = g\beta_M JH/kT$ and

$$B_J(x) = \frac{2J+1}{2J} \coth \frac{(2J+1)x}{2J} - \frac{1}{2J} \coth \frac{x}{2J} \qquad (3\text{--}22)$$

is known as the *Brillouin function*. It is found that for fields of the order of 10^4 gauss, $g\beta_M H/k$ is of the order of $1°K$, so that for moderate temperatures the exponentials can be expanded, and we obtain as an approximation,

$$M_z = \frac{NJ(J+1)g^2\beta_M{}^2 H}{3kT}$$

We recall that $M_z = \chi_v H$, so the *static Curie susceptibility*, designated by χ_0, is

$$\chi_0 = \frac{N g^2 \beta_M^2 J(J + 1)}{3kT} \qquad (3\text{--}23)$$

Let us now assume that we need only to consider the moment due to the spin (as we shall see later, this is frequently the case because of the "quenching" of the orbital moment). The magnetic moment of an electron, due to its spin, is given by $2\sqrt{s(s + 1)}\beta_M$, which is analogous to Eq. 2–38 if it is recalled that the moment is twice as large as that caused by orbital motion. For a species composed of several unpaired electrons, we write

$$\mu_s = 2\sqrt{S(S + 1)}\beta_M \qquad (3\text{--}24)$$

where $S = \sum_i s_i$. In this case, $J = S$, and noting also that $g = 2$, Eq. 3–23 becomes

$$\chi_0 = \frac{N \mu_s^2}{3kT} \qquad (3\text{--}25)$$

which is the well-known *Langevin equation*. We note the temperature dependence of this susceptibility, in confirmation of our previous statement, and note also that the paramagnetic susceptibility is 10^2 to 10^3 times larger and of opposite sign when compared with the diamagnetic susceptibility previously considered.

Equation 3–25 is frequently used to interpret magnetic-susceptibility data in terms of the number of unpaired electrons present. Stable paramagnetic species are confined pretty well to the transition and inner transition elements, although not exclusively. All species which contain an odd number of electrons are, of course, paramagnetic, but paramagnetism is found among those with even numbers as well. *Hund's rules* can be used to determine the nature of the atomic state which arises from a given electronic configuration:

1. Assign the maximum value of S consistent with the Pauli principle.
2. Assign the maximum value of L consistent with S.
3. $J = L - S$ for shells that are less than half filled, and $J = L + S$ for shells that are more than half filled.

These rules are very useful because the specification of the atomic structure is of utmost importance as a starting point for most problems in chemical structure. Although Hund's rules were originally formulated on the basis of empirical spectroscopic observations, they can now be justified in terms of our wave-mechanical model of the atom.

A similar paramagnetism is associated with the permanent nuclear moments. In this case we write in place of Eq. 3–20

$$M_z = \frac{N \sum\limits_{m=-I}^{+I} g_N \beta_N m e^{g_N \beta_N H m / kT}}{\sum\limits_{m=-I}^{+I} e^{g_N \beta_N H m / kT}} \tag{3–26}$$

Since nuclear moments are so much smaller than electronic moments, we can immediately expand the exponentials in Eq. 3–26 to obtain

$$M_z = \frac{N \sum\limits_{m=-I}^{+I} g_N \beta_N m (1 + g_N \beta_N H m / kT)}{\sum\limits_{m=-I}^{+I} (1 + g_N \beta_N H m / kT)}$$

$$= \frac{N \sum\limits_{m=-I}^{+I} (g_N \beta_N m kT + g_N^2 \beta_N^2 H m^2)}{\sum\limits_{m=-I}^{+I} (kT + g_N \beta_N H m)} = \frac{N g_N^2 \beta_N^2 H \sum\limits_{m=-I}^{+I} m^2}{kT \sum\limits_{m=-I}^{+I} 1}$$

since terms which are linear in m will obviously contribute nothing to a sum in which m takes on all values from $-I$ to $+I$. Using

$$\sum\limits_{m=-I}^{+I} 1 = 2I + 1 \quad \text{and} \quad \sum\limits_{m=-I}^{+I} m^2 = \tfrac{1}{3} I(I + 1)(2I + 1)$$

we obtain

$$M_z = \frac{(I + 1) N \mu^2 H}{3 I k T}$$

from which,

$$\chi_n = \frac{M_z}{H} = \frac{(I + 1) N \mu^2}{3 I k T} \tag{3–27}$$

The nuclear paramagnetism is very small. For example, it is of the order of 10^{-10} for the protons in water at room temperature and this is completely masked by the electronic diamagnetic susceptibility which is of the order of 10^{-6}. Because of the inverse temperature dependence, nuclear paramagnetism can be observed at low temperatures. This has been done, for example, in solid hydrogen near absolute zero.

3–2   THE MAGNETIC RESONANCE METHOD

The fundamentals of the magnetic resonance phenomenon can be adequately described in classical as well as quantum-mechanical terms.

Certain aspects of each are worthy of consideration here, so we will discuss the classical theory, followed by a brief quantum-mechanical description.

Classical Description

Let us consider the effect of the magnetic field upon a given magnetic moment in the sample.[1] When a magnetic moment is placed in a uniform magnetic field, a torque is exerted on it which tends to align it perpendicular to the field:

$$\mathbf{L} = \boldsymbol{\mu} \times \mathbf{H} \tag{3-28}$$

By Newton's laws this torque produces an angular acceleration,

$$\frac{d\mathbf{M}}{dt} = \boldsymbol{\mu} \times \mathbf{H}$$

which, by virtue of our discussion in Sec. 2–4, can be written as

$$\frac{d\boldsymbol{\mu}}{dt} = \gamma \boldsymbol{\mu} \times \mathbf{H} \tag{3-29}$$

With $\mathbf{H}$ taken to be in the z-direction, this is equivalent to the three equations,

$$\frac{d\mu_x}{dt} = \gamma \mu_y H \tag{3-30a}$$

$$\frac{d\mu_y}{dt} = -\gamma \mu_x H \tag{3-30b}$$

$$\frac{d\mu_z}{dt} = 0 \tag{3-30c}$$

From Eq. 3–30c we conclude that μ_z is constant. If we define α as the angle that $\boldsymbol{\mu}$ makes with the z-axis, then

$$\mu_z = \mu \cos \alpha \tag{3-31}$$

The coupled differential equations, Eqs. 3–30a and 3–30b can readily be separated by differentiation. Thus,

$$\frac{d^2\mu_x}{dt^2} = \gamma H \frac{d\mu_y}{dt} = -\gamma^2 H^2 \mu_x \tag{3-32}$$

---

[1] This problem is analogous to that treated in Sec. 3–1, p. 35, and the solution is thus somewhat repetitious. An alternative solution is given here, however, which may give the reader more insight.

with an equation of identical form for μ_y. Solutions for such equations are well known; they are of the form,

$$\mu_x = A \cos \gamma Ht + B \sin \gamma Ht$$
$$\mu_y = C \cos \gamma Ht + D \sin \gamma Ht \tag{3-33}$$

Because of the coupled nature of the original equations, the coefficients A, B, C, D cannot be chosen arbitrarily. Putting solutions 3–33 into Eq. 3–30a requires that

$$-\gamma HA \sin \gamma Ht + \gamma HB \cos \gamma Ht = \gamma HC \cos \gamma Ht + \gamma HD \sin \gamma Ht$$

or

$$(B - C) \cos \gamma Ht = (A + D) \sin \gamma Ht$$

Thus, the sine and cosine terms are not independent, and for a particular choice of phase we obtain,

$$\mu_x = (\text{const}) \cos \gamma Ht$$
$$\mu_y = -(\text{const}) \sin \gamma Ht$$

The constant is readily evaluated from

$$\mu_x{}^2 + \mu_y{}^2 + \mu_z{}^2 = \mu^2$$
$$(\text{const})^2 \cos^2 \gamma Ht + (\text{const})^2 \sin^2 \gamma Ht + \mu^2 \cos^2 \alpha = \mu^2$$

which is obviously satisfied by

$$\text{const} = \mu \sin \alpha$$

The solutions are

$$\mu_x = \mu \sin \alpha \cos \gamma Ht$$
$$\mu_y = -\mu \sin \alpha \sin \gamma Ht \tag{3-34}$$
$$\mu_z = \mu \cos \alpha$$

It can readily be verified that these equations describe a circular motion about the z-axis of angular velocity $\omega = -\gamma H$, in accordance with Eq. 3–10. It is customary in magnetic resonance spectroscopy to designate the strong polarizing field in the z-direction by $\mathbf{H_0}$. Then

$$\boldsymbol{\omega_0} = -\gamma \mathbf{H_0} \tag{3-35}$$

This motion is depicted schematically in Fig. 3–3.

It is convenient to view this motion from a system of coordinates which is rotating about the magnetic-field direction with an angular velocity ω. Using

$$\frac{d\boldsymbol{\mu}}{dt} = -\gamma \mathbf{H_0} \times \boldsymbol{\mu}$$

in (see Eq. 3–6)

$$\left(\frac{d\boldsymbol{\mu}}{dt}\right)_s = \left(\frac{d\boldsymbol{\mu}}{dt}\right)_b + \boldsymbol{\omega} \times \boldsymbol{\mu}$$

we obtain

$$\left(\frac{d\boldsymbol{\mu}}{dt}\right)_b = -\gamma \mathbf{H}_0 \times \boldsymbol{\mu} + \boldsymbol{\mu} \times \boldsymbol{\omega} = -\gamma \left(\mathbf{H}_0 + \frac{\boldsymbol{\omega}}{\gamma}\right) \times \boldsymbol{\mu} \qquad (3\text{–}36)$$

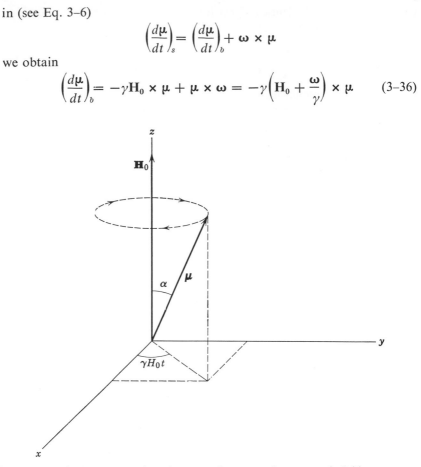

Fig. 3–3   Precession of a magnetic moment in a magnetic field.

Thus, in the rotating frame it appears that the magnetic moment is responding to an effective field,

$$\mathbf{H}_0 + \frac{\boldsymbol{\omega}}{\gamma}$$

When $\boldsymbol{\omega} = \boldsymbol{\omega}_0 = -\gamma \mathbf{H}_0$, the effective field is zero and the magnetic moment is a constant vector in this rotating coordinate system.

We now consider the effect of an additional small, linearly oscillating field in the xy-plane, which we can arbitrarily assume to define the x-axis. It is convenient to think of this field as the resultant of two counter-circulating components of magnitude H_1 which add together vectorially to give the linear oscillation whose amplitude is $2H_1$ (see Fig. 3–4). In a frame which is rotating at the same angular velocity as the components of the H_1 field, the effective field

$$\mathbf{H}_e = \mathbf{H}_0 + \mathbf{H}_1 + \frac{\omega}{\gamma} \qquad (3\text{--}37)$$

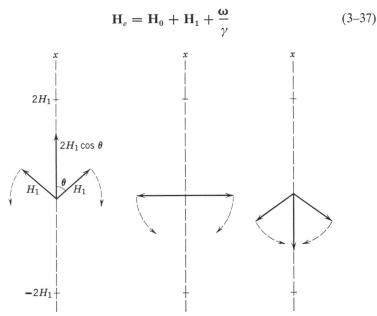

Fig. 3–4   Resolution of a linear oscillation into circulating components.

is obviously constant, and we write as an equation of motion for $\boldsymbol{\mu}$ in this rotating frame,

$$\frac{d\boldsymbol{\mu}}{dt} = -\gamma \mathbf{H}_e \times \boldsymbol{\mu}$$

This equation is of the same form as that previously encountered, and we conclude that $\boldsymbol{\mu}$ precesses about $\mathbf{H}_e$, which is itself precessing about the strong $\mathbf{H}_0$ field direction. Figure 3–5 is an attempt to illustrate this motion.

If it is assumed at time $t = 0$ that $\boldsymbol{\mu}$ is along the strong field direction, at a later time t it is found that

$$\frac{\mu_z}{|\boldsymbol{\mu}|} = \cos \alpha = 1 - 2 \sin^2 \theta \sin^2 \tfrac{1}{2}\omega't \qquad (3\text{--}38)$$

where θ is the angle which the effective field $\mathbf{H}_e$ makes with respect to $\mathbf{H}_0$, and ω' is the precessional frequency of $\boldsymbol{\mu}$ about $\mathbf{H}_e$. We find that

$$\sin^2 \theta = \left(\frac{|\mathbf{H}_1|}{|\mathbf{H}_e|}\right)^2 = \frac{H_1^{\,2}}{H_1^{\,2} + (H_0 + \omega/\gamma)^2} \qquad (3\text{--}39)$$

and

$$\omega' = -\gamma H_e = -\gamma \left[H_1{}^2 + \left(H_0 + \frac{\omega}{\gamma} \right)^2 \right]^{\frac{1}{2}} \qquad (3\text{-}40)$$

Thus, the orientation of $\boldsymbol{\mu}$ with respect to $\mathbf{H_0}$ is given by

$$\cos \alpha = 1 - \frac{2H_1{}^2}{H_1{}^2 + (H_0 + \omega/\gamma)^2} \sin^2 \left\{ \frac{t}{2} [(\gamma H_1)^2 + (\gamma H_0 + \omega)^2]^{\frac{1}{2}} \right\} \quad (3\text{-}41)$$

Classically, the angular momentum can assume any orientation in space, and its z-component is simply $\mu \cos \alpha$. Since the spin and magnetic moment are linearly related, similar considerations apply. Let us consider in particular the case of spin $\frac{1}{2}$. If $P_{\frac{1}{2}}$ and $P_{-\frac{1}{2}}$ are the probabilities that the z-component of spin is $\frac{1}{2}$ or $-\frac{1}{2}$ respectively, then

$$\tfrac{1}{2} \cos \alpha = \tfrac{1}{2} P_{\frac{1}{2}} + -\tfrac{1}{2} P_{-\frac{1}{2}} \quad (3\text{-}42)$$

However, since $P_{\frac{1}{2}} + P_{-\frac{1}{2}} = 1$, we have

$$P_{-\frac{1}{2}} = \frac{1 - \cos \alpha}{2}$$

Using Eq. 3–41,

$$P_{-\frac{1}{2}} = 1 - P_{\frac{1}{2}}$$

$$= \left[\frac{H_1{}^2}{H_1{}^2 + (H_0 + \omega/\gamma)^2} \right] \sin^2 \left\{ \frac{t}{2} [(\gamma H_1)^2 + (\gamma H_0 + \omega)^2]^{\frac{1}{2}} \right\} \quad (3\text{-}43)$$

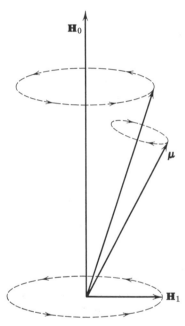

Fig. 3–5 Precession of a magnetic moment in a static plus rotating magnetic field.

If the frequency of the $\mathbf{H_1}$ field is such that $\boldsymbol{\omega} = -\gamma \mathbf{H_0}$, then $\mathbf{H_e} = \mathbf{H_1}$ and $\theta = \pi/2$. In this case Eq. 3–43 becomes

$$P_{-\frac{1}{2}} = 1 - P_{\frac{1}{2}} = \sin^2 \frac{\gamma H_1 t}{2}$$

$$= \tfrac{1}{2}(1 - \cos \gamma H_1 t) \quad (3\text{-}43a)$$

and the system can be regarded as oscillating wildly between spins $\frac{1}{2}$ and $-\frac{1}{2}$ at the resonance condition. We have entirely neglected the other component of the oscillating field thus far. Because it is rotating in the opposite sense, it will be far from fulfilling the resonance condition and will exert only a very small perturbation which can be evaluated by using Eq. 3–43.

On a macroscopic scale, the magnetization behaves in the same way as the individual moments, provided that each is subjected to the same magnetic fields.

Quantum-Mechanical Description

We have seen that the energy of charged particles with nonvanishing angular momenta is independent of the quantum number m, and is therefore $(2F + 1)$-fold degenerate, where F is the azimuthal quantum number.[1] In a magnetic field, this degeneracy is removed in accordance with Eq. 3–16, and splittings such as those illustrated for $F = \frac{1}{2}$ and $F = \frac{3}{2}$ in

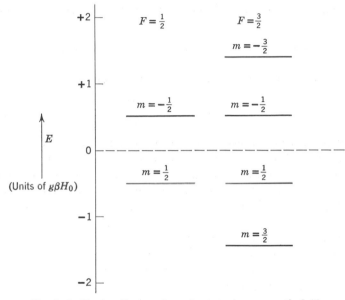

Fig. 3–6   Energy diagram for spin states in a magnetic field.

Fig. 3–6 are obtained. With the system quantized with respect to the z-axis, a small oscillating field along the x-direction is added. The energy of this additional interaction is

$$\mathbf{E} = -\boldsymbol{\mu} \cdot \mathbf{H}$$
$$= 2\mu_x H_1 \cos \omega t$$
$$= 2\gamma \hbar H_1 F_x \cos \omega t$$

where the amplitude of the oscillating field has been assumed to be $2H_1$, and its frequency is $\nu = \omega/2\pi$. It is this interaction which induces transitions among the quantized energy states. The probability of such transitions is found by constructing the Hamiltonian operator for the preceding interaction, and evaluating matrix elements which link the two states

[1] F is used here as a more general quantum number, denoting I or J respectively, depending on whether nuclei or electrons are being discussed.

involved. The result is

$$P_{mm'} = \gamma^2 H_1^2 \, |\langle \psi_{m'}| \, \hat{F}_x \, |\psi_m \rangle|^2 \, \delta(\omega_0 - \omega) \qquad (3\text{-}44)$$

where ψ_m is the stationary-state wave function for the energy level characterized by the quantum number m and $\delta(\omega_0 - \omega)$ is the *Dirac delta function*. The latter quantity is defined as being zero everywhere except at $\omega = \omega_0$, which is another way of saying that infinitesimally sharp transitions are predicted quantum-mechanically. Using previously derived relationships, the difference in energy between the m and m' states is

$$h\nu_0 = |E_{m'} - E_m| = |m' - m| \, g\beta H_0 = |m' - m| \, \frac{\mu H_0}{F}$$

and since $\omega_0 = 2\pi\nu_0$, the angular velocity of a transition is

$$\omega_0 = |m' - m| \, \frac{\mu H_0}{\hbar F} \qquad (3\text{-}45)$$

The matrix elements occurring in Eq. 3–44 can be evaluated with Eqs. 2–37, and it is found that $\langle m'| \, \hat{F}_x \, |m \rangle = 0$ unless $m' = m \pm 1$. Thus, the *selection rule* for transitions is $\Delta m = \pm 1$; that is, only single-quantum transitions are allowed. It should also be noted that the transition probability turns out to be symmetric with respect to an interchange of the quantum numbers ($P_{m'm} = P_{mm'}$). Note that it is the *probability* of a transition between two states which is equal rather than the *number* of transitions. It will be recalled that there is a population difference between the states given by the Boltzmann factor, $e^{-\mu H_0/FkT}$, so that with an equal transition probability, there are more transitions from the lower energy state than from the upper. Thus, there is a net change in the magnetization when the resonance condition is fulfilled. Otherwise, there would be no net change in a sample, and the resonance would not be observable.

The infinitesimally sharp transition at $\omega = \omega_0$ is appropriate only for a single, isolated particle, and this, of course, is never found in actual practice. There are many factors which tend to broaden the resonance signals, the most important being the following:

Spontaneous emission. In addition to the induced transitions previously described, transitions from the upper state can take place by the spontaneous radiative emission of a quantum of energy. If the natural lifetime of the upper state is Δt, then, from the Heisenberg uncertainty principle, the natural width of the energy level is

$$\Delta E \approx \frac{\hbar}{\Delta t} \qquad (3\text{-}46)$$

and, because $\Delta E = h\Delta\nu$, ω is distributed over the range,

$$\Delta\omega \approx \frac{1}{\Delta t} \tag{3-47}$$

Thus, if spontaneous emission takes place sufficiently often, a broadened resonance is observed, although it is usually found that the other effects mentioned in the following predominate.

Spin-lattice relaxation. Because this effect is discussed in detail later (see Sec. 3–3, p. 53), we merely note here that the lifetime of the upper state can also be determined by the rate of energy exchange with the other degrees of freedom in the sample, such as vibrations and rotations. All other energy states with which the spin system can exchange energy are referred to collectively as the *lattice*, although they are often confined to the single molecular entity containing the magnetic moment of interest.

Spin-spin relaxation. This form is also given only brief mention at this point, for it is discussed in a subsequent section (see Sec. 3–3, p. 58). In solid samples and viscous liquids neighboring magnetic moments remain fixed in position for long periods of time, and they can alter the local field at various points in the sample through dipolar interactions. These interactions shorten the lifetime of the excited state by allowing an energy exchange to take place within the spin system.

Unresolved hyperfine interactions. Interactions between magnetic moments also take place in such a way that there are isotropic components which do not vanish with rapid reorientation of the molecules. This gives rise to spin multiplets, the nature of which will constitute the subject matter of many of our later discussions. These interactions are sometimes small so that the multiplet structure of the absorption is not clearly resolved and the peak appears to be broadened.

Nuclear quadrupole interactions. As previously mentioned, nuclei with spin greater than $\frac{1}{2}$ can possess electric-quadrupole moments, which can interact with an electric field, provided it has a nonvanishing gradient at the nucleus. This provides another means of energy exchange between the spin system and the lattice and leads to an additional broadening by decreasing the lifetime of the upper state.

Instrumental broadening. Last, but not least, a magnetic resonance signal may be broadened because the various molecules of which the sample is composed experience slightly different external magnetic fields, or there may be imperfections in the phase-sensitive selection used to detect the signal. These instrumental difficulties give broadened resonances which are not always symmetrical. They are strictly experimental problems, but they can be the most important considerations in actual practice.

The discussion leading up to Eq. 3–44 is appropriate only for a single, isolated moment, and cannot be easily generalized to include the afore-mentioned broadening features. However, we can use the general features quoted previously, and introduce in a phenomenological way a line-shape function $g(\omega)$ to replace the Dirac delta function in Eq. 3–44:

$$P_{mm'} = \gamma^2 H_1^2 \, |\langle \psi_{m'} | \, \hat{F}_x \, | \psi_m \rangle|^2 \, g(\omega) \qquad (3\text{–}48)$$

We note that here, as in Eq. 3–44, the line-shape function has the dimension of time, being proportional to the power absorbed at the angular velocity ω. The actual form of $g(\omega)$ will depend upon the nature of the broadening mechanism which predominates in a particular case.

Finally, we should note that the classical and quantum-mechanical theories of the magnetic resonance phenomenon are entirely equivalent, except, obviously, for the quantization of angular momentum. Although we have only sketched the main features here of the quantum treatment, we can solve the time-dependent Schrödinger equation for the motion of a magnetic moment in a variable magnetic field. This has been done by Rabi and Schwinger, who have shown that the result is Eq. 3–43.

3–3   RELAXATION PHENOMENA

As we have seen, induced transitions occur with equal probability in both directions between a pair of energy states, and spontaneous transi-tions can be neglected in most cases. Now a magnetic resonance signal can be observed only if there is a change in the magnetization of the sample accompanying the absorption of energy from the rotating H_1 field. Thus, we conclude that the change in magnetization is due entirely to the inequality of the population distribution among the Zeeman levels.[1] A numerical evaluation of this population difference with the use of the Boltzmann equation shows that it is quite small (of the order of one part in 10^3 to 10^5) in the moderate fields of about 10,000 gauss which are used in most magnetic resonance spectroscopy experiments. However, it is these very small changes in population which are of concern to us.

It is quite obvious that a magnetic resonance signal should soon disappear at the resonance condition. This follows from the fact that there are more transitions from the lower state than from the upper because of the population difference. This difference is decreased and

[1] The splitting up of electronic energy levels in a magnetic field is known as the Zeeman effect. The analogous removal of the nuclear-spin degeneracy in the presence of a magnetic field is often referred to as a nuclear Zeeman effect.

the magnetization vanishes as an even distribution among the spin states is achieved. In terms of the $F = \frac{1}{2}$ case previously considered, this means that the simple sinusoidal behavior of $P_{\frac{1}{2}}$ and $P_{-\frac{1}{2}}$ (see Eq. 3–43a) is quickly damped to $P_{\frac{1}{2}} = P_{-\frac{1}{2}} = \frac{1}{2}$ at the resonance condition.

There are other mechanisms which need to be considered, some of which tend to restore the thermal equilibrium among the spin states so that a net absorption of energy can be observed. We refer to the processes by which the equilibrium condition is restored as *relaxation* phenomena. It is necessary to consider two entirely different mechanisms of relaxation in magnetic resonance spectroscopy, the nature of which will be discussed in the following.

Spin-Lattice Relaxation

Spin-lattice relaxation is the process of maintaining thermal equilibrium in the spin system through energy exchange with the normal thermal motions of the molecule and the surrounding molecules. This thermal contact is a result of interactions of the magnetic moments with random, fluctuating magnetic fields, the latter being a result of the thermal motions of the nuclei in the molecule. A component of the fluctuating field which happens to be at the Larmor frequency for a particular value of the polarizing field induces transitions among the energy levels and thus restores the thermal distribution.

It will be useful to continue thinking in terms of the spin $\frac{1}{2}$ case to which we previously referred. The system is thought of as having been brought to an even distribution ($P_{\frac{1}{2}} = P_{-\frac{1}{2}} = \frac{1}{2}$) by resonance absorption. Since the probabilities of upward and downward transitions are equal, how can the system be restored to thermal equilibrium? The answer to this question is by no means obvious, but can be visualized as follows:

We define n_+ as the population of the lower ($+\frac{1}{2}$) state, and n_- as the population of the upper ($-\frac{1}{2}$) state (see Fig. 3–6). If W_+ is the probability of an upward transition and W_- is the probability of a downward transition, then $n_+ W_+$ is the number of upward transitions, and $n_- W_-$ is the number of transitions downward. Initially, $n_+ = n_-$, but at equilibrium,

$$(n_+ W_+)_{\text{eq}} = (n_- W_-)_{\text{eq}} \qquad (3\text{--}49)$$

or, by the Boltzmann factor,

$$\frac{W_+}{W_-} = \left(\frac{n_-}{n_+}\right)_{\text{eq}} = e^{-2\mu H_0 / kT} \qquad (3\text{--}50)$$

This appears to be a contradiction to our foregoing statement concerning the equality of the transitions probabilities. There is a difference, however. We consider in the present case a *coupled* thermal and spin system. Conservation of energy requires that, for every upward transition in the spin system, there is a downward transition in the lattice, and vice versa. There is not a complete equivalence in upward and downward transitions which can occur in the lattice, however.

Although similar considerations apply to any number of degrees of freedom of the lattice, we will illustrate this inequality for the specific case of vibrational motion. Assume a set of harmonic oscillators, each with a characteristic frequency $v_0 = \omega_0/2\pi = 2\mu H_0/h$. As is well known, each oscillator can have any of the quantized values of the energy,

$$E_v = (v + \tfrac{1}{2})hv_0$$

where v is a quantum number which is restricted to zero and positive integral values. We can describe this system of oscillators by a set of population numbers N_v, defined by

$$N_v = Ce^{-vhv_0/kT}$$

where C is a constant. N_v can thus be taken to be the number of oscillators having vibrational energy $(v + \tfrac{1}{2})hv_0$.

For downward transitions in the spin system, we require that corresponding upward transitions take place in the lattice system. We assume that all these occur with equal probability, so W_- is simply proportional to the number of oscillators available for an upward lattice transition. If this proportionality constant is taken to be B, then

$$W_- = B\sum_{v=0}^{\infty} N_v = BC\sum_{v=0}^{\infty} e^{-vhv_0/kT}$$

Similarly, W_+ is related to the number of oscillators which are available for downward lattice transitions. However, since downward transitions are not possible from the $v = 0$ energy level, we write

$$W_+ = B\sum_{v=1}^{\infty} N_v = BC\sum_{v=1}^{\infty} e^{-vhv_0/kT}$$

The ratio gives

$$\frac{W_+}{W_-} = \frac{\sum_{v=1}^{\infty} e^{-vhv_0/kT}}{\sum_{v=0}^{\infty} e^{-vhv_0/kT}} = \frac{e^{-hv_0/kT} + e^{-2hv_0/kT} + e^{-3hv_0/kT} + \cdots}{1 + e^{-hv_0/kT} + e^{-2hv_0/kT} + e^{-3hv_0/kT} + \cdots}$$

$$= \frac{e^{-hv_0/kT}(1 + e^{-hv_0/kT} + e^{-2hv_0/kT} + \cdots)}{1 + e^{-hv_0/kT} + e^{-2hv_0/kT} + \cdots} = e^{-hv_0/kT}$$

which is completely equivalent to Eq. 3–50 if it is recalled that $hv_0 = 2\mu H_0$. Thus, transitions in the spin system which are "tied" to transitions in the lattice do not occur with equal probability, and this coupling with the lattice degrees of freedom will tend to counteract any displacement of the spin system from the equilibrium thermal distribution.

Let us now assume that we have a system which has been perturbed from the equilibrium condition, and investigate the rate at which it returns to a thermal distribution among the energy states. Except at extremely low temperatures, the exponential term in Eq. 3–50 is near unity, as we previously noted, and it is convenient to define a transition probability W in terms of the equations

$$W_- = We^{\mu H_0/kT} = W\left(1 + \frac{\mu H_0}{kT} + \frac{1}{2!}\frac{\mu^2 H_0^2}{k^2 T^2} + \cdots\right) \approx W\left(1 + \frac{\mu H_0}{kT}\right)$$

$$(3-51)$$

$$W_+ = We^{-\mu H_0/kT} = W\left(1 - \frac{\mu H_0}{kT} + \frac{1}{2!}\frac{\mu^2 H_0^2}{k^2 T^2} + \cdots\right) \approx W\left(1 - \frac{\mu H_0}{kT}\right)$$

Similarly,

$$(n_+)_{eq} = \frac{N}{2} e^{\mu H_0/kT} \approx \frac{N}{2}\left(1 + \frac{\mu H_0}{kT}\right)$$

$$(n_-)_{eq} = \frac{N}{2} e^{-\mu H_0/kT} \approx \frac{N}{2}\left(1 - \frac{\mu H_0}{kT}\right)$$

$$(3-52)$$

where $N = n_+ + n_-$.

The rate at which the population of the states changes is given by

$$\frac{dn_+}{dt} = -\frac{dn_-}{dt} = n_- W_- - n_+ W_+$$

$$= W(n_- e^{\mu H_0/kT} - n_+ e^{-\mu H_0/kT}) \qquad (3-53)$$

It is more convenient to solve for the rate of change of the population difference, $n_+ - n_- \equiv n$. Since n changes by two for each transition, we write

$$\frac{dn}{dt} = 2W(n_- e^{\mu H_0/kT} - n_+ e^{-\mu H_0/kT})$$

$$\approx 2W\left[n_-\left(1 + \frac{\mu H_0}{kT}\right) - n_+\left(1 - \frac{\mu H_0}{kT}\right)\right]$$

or,

$$\frac{dn}{dt} = 2W(n_{eq} - n) \qquad (3-54)$$

We have used the definition $n_{eq} \equiv (n_+ - n_-)_{eq} = N(\mu H_0/kT)$ (see Eq. 3–52) in writing Eq. 3–54.

Equation 3–54 is a simple first-order rate equation which can be readily integrated to give

$$2Wt = \ln \frac{n_{eq} - n_0}{n_{eq} - n} \qquad (3\text{--}55)$$

where n_0 is the initial value of n. Equation 3–55 can also be written as

$$n = n_{eq}\left(1 - \frac{n_{eq} - n_0}{n_{eq}} e^{-2Wt}\right) \qquad (3\text{--}56)$$

In this form it is immediately apparent that n decays exponentially from its initial value n_0 at time $t = 0$ to the equilibrium value n_{eq} at time $t = \infty$ with a characteristic time constant $1/2W$. We define this time constant as the *spin-lattice relaxation time*,

$$T_1 = \frac{1}{2W} \qquad (3\text{--}57)$$

The experimental determination of T_1 depends on the fact that M_z, the total magnetization in the z-direction, is just $n\mu$. Thus, on a macroscopic scale, we write as an equation analogous to Eq. 3–54,

$$\frac{dM_z}{dt} = \frac{1}{T_1}(M_{z,eq} - M_z) \qquad (3\text{--}58)$$

and T_1 can be determined by observing the exponential decay of a magnetic resonance signal as a function of time after the H_1 field has been turned off. It is found that T_1 varies all the way from $\sim 10^{-5}$ sec in solutions to several hours in low-temperature crystals.

The essential features of the spin-lattice-relaxation process emerged from the fundamental work of Bloembergen, Purcell, and Pound, although more general formulations of the theory have been given by Wangsness and Bloch, and by Redfield. Much of the current literature of magnetic resonance spectroscopy, e.g., the Redfield theory, is phrased in terms of *density matrices*. Although a general discussion would take us too far afield, we can easily sketch the basic concept of a density matrix. We have remarked (see Sec. 2–1) that the only observable values of a dynamical variable are given by an eigenvalue equation, and it is often convenient to express the state function for a system in terms of the eigenfunctions of a particular operator. For example, if Ψ is a normalized state function, and we wish to calculate the expectation value of M_z, we write (see Eq. 2-4),

$$\bar{M}_z = \langle \Psi | \, \hat{M}_z \, | \Psi \rangle$$
$$= \sum_{j,k} c_j^* c_k \langle \psi_j | \, \hat{M}_z \, | \psi_k \rangle$$

where

$$\Psi = \sum_i c_i \psi_i$$

and the ψ_i are regarded as stationary solutions of the wave equation, $\hat{H}\psi_i = E_i\psi_i$. Within this manifold of states, the matrix elements

$$\langle \psi_j | \, \hat{M}_z \, | \psi_k \rangle$$

are all constants, so that if $\bar{M}_z$ is a function of time, as it often is, the time dependence must be expressed by variation of the coefficients c_i. The quantities $c_j^* c_k$ form a matrix $\boldsymbol{\rho}$, called the density matrix, whose elements are defined by

$$\rho_{jk} = \langle \psi_j | \, \hat{\rho} \, | \psi_k \rangle = c_j^* c_k$$

It is readily found that $\hat{\rho}$ must satisfy the differential equation,

$$\frac{d\hat{\rho}}{dt} = \frac{i}{\hbar} (\hat{\rho}\hat{H} - \hat{H}\hat{\rho})$$

which, in the simple case where $\hat{H}$ does not depend on time, leads to

$$\rho_{jk}(t) = \exp\left[-\frac{i}{\hbar}(E_j - E_k)t \right] \rho_{jk}(0)$$

for the matrix elements of $\hat{\rho}$ at time t in terms of those at time $t = 0$. These results can be alternatively formulated by a perturbation theory calculation in which a time dependence of the c_i's is considered, but the density-matrix method yields a formulation which is particularly useful. A good introductory discussion of density matrices can be found in Ref. 9.

Another concept often used in the discussion of spin-lattice relaxation is that of a *spin temperature*, which is defined for the $F = \frac{1}{2}$ case by

$$\frac{n_+}{n_-} = e^{2\mu H_0 / kT_s} \approx 1 + \frac{2\mu H_0}{kT_s} \tag{3-59}$$

We should point out that the spin temperature (like any other temperature) is defined only for quasi-equilibrium conditions. Obviously, at thermal equilibrium $T_s = T$, and spin-lattice relaxation can be described as the process by which two thermodynamic assemblies in contact with one another achieve the same equilibrium temperature. If $n > n_{eq}$, we say that the spin temperature is greater than the lattice temperature. Just as when $T = \infty$ in the thermal case, $T_s = \infty$ corresponds to an even distribution among the spin states ($n = 0$). It is possible to polarize the sample in certain experiments in such a way that $n < n_{eq}$; in this case, we speak of a negative spin temperature. Note that T and T_s are *temperatures*, whereas T_1 and T_2 (to be defined in the next section) are *time constants*.

Spin-Spin Relaxation

As the name implies, we are concerned here with a relaxation process in which the energy exchanges are confined entirely to the spin system. To illustrate the process, let us consider a situation in which we have the resonance condition fulfilled by a continuously applied H_1 field rotating at the Larmor frequency $\omega_0 = -\gamma H_0$. In terms of the classical viewpoint developed previously, we think of a precessional motion of the magnetic moments about the polarizing field, H_0. With H_1 applied for a sufficient period of time, the individual moments will be drawn into phase, and all precess about H_0 together. If the H_1 field is now removed, the moments will continue to precess about H_0, and the magnetization will slowly change to its equilibrium value in a time characteristic of the spin-lattice-relaxation process.

The decay of the magnetic resonance signal may be more rapid, however, if there are neighboring magnetic moments in the sample. Unless these moments move about rapidly, they will make small, local contributions to the magnetic field, so the field can be regarded as inhomogeneous on a microscopic scale. As a result, the individual magnetic moments precess in fields of slightly different strength, and they will quickly lose phase because of the difference in their precessional frequencies. If the interaction between these magnetic moments, or spins, is such that a range of magnetic fields ΔH_0 is produced, then the precessional frequencies vary in the range $\Delta \omega_0 = -\gamma \Delta H_0$. The reciprocal of $\Delta \omega_0$ has the dimension of time and serves as a measure of the length of time required for this dephasing to occur. Quantitatively, we define the *spin-spin relaxation time* by

$$T_2 = \frac{1}{\Delta \omega_0} = -\frac{1}{\gamma \Delta H_0} \tag{3-60}$$

An alternative definition of T_2 is often given. As previously mentioned, magnetic resonance absorption occurs over a range of frequencies owing to the microscopic field inhomogeneity resulting from spin-spin interactions. Hence, there is an intimate connection between the line-shape function and the spin-spin relaxation time. The exact relationship is

$$T_2 = \tfrac{1}{2}[g(\omega)]_{max} \tag{3-61}$$

where $[g(\omega)]_{max}$ is the maximum value of the line-shape function introduced in Sec. 3-2, p. 52. The reason for this particular choice will be apparent when we discuss the Bloch equations (Sec. 3-4).

Saturation

We have discussed two effects that work against one another to determine the distribution among the spin states under resonance conditions. The first of these is the tendency toward an infinite spin temperature caused by the inducement of transitions between the spin states by the H_1 field. The probability of such transitions is given by Eq. 3-48. If we represent this transition probability simply by P, then the net rate of change of population between the states by induced transitions is

$$P(n_+ - n_-) = Pn$$

The second effect we have discussed is relaxation, which tends to restore the equilibrium distribution. If the relaxation time is small, a signal can be readily observed; whereas if the relaxation time is large, the spin system heats up faster than it can be cooled down by thermal exchange with the lattice, and the magnetic resonance signal decays to zero as the spin temperature is raised. This phenomenon is termed *saturation*.

We can discuss saturation more quantitatively by combining the rate of population change for induced transitions with that for spin-lattice relaxation (Eq. 3-54). Recalling again that each single transition changes the population difference by two, we write

$$\frac{dn}{dt} = \frac{n_{eq} - n}{T_1} - 2nP = \frac{n_{eq}}{T_1} - \frac{1 + 2PT_1}{T_1}n \qquad (3\text{-}62)$$

Integration of this equation as before yields,

$$n = \frac{n_{eq}}{1 + 2PT_1} + \left(n_i - \frac{n_{eq}}{1 + 2PT_1}\right)e^{[(1+2PT_1)^t/T_1]}$$

Thus n approaches the value

$$\frac{n_{eq}}{1 + 2PT_1}$$

at time $t = \infty$, and the characteristic time constant for this first-order process is

$$\frac{T_1}{1 + 2PT_1}$$

We see that both the equilibrium value of n and the time constant which characterizes the approach to equilibrium are decreased by the factor,

$$\frac{1}{1 + 2PT_1} \tag{3-63}$$

which is known as the *saturation factor*. We have previously noted that the only allowed transitions are $\Delta m = \pm 1$. Using Eq. 2–37 to evaluate the integrals occurring in Eq. 3–48, we find that $P = \frac{1}{4}\gamma^2 H_1^2 g(\omega)$ for our case of $F = \frac{1}{2}$. The saturation factor for the spin $\frac{1}{2}$ case is thus

$$\frac{1}{1 + \frac{1}{2}\gamma^2 H_1^2 T_1 g(\omega)} \tag{3-64}$$

It will be observed that the greatest degree of saturation, or the greatest reduction in the magnetic resonance signal, occurs at the maximum value of $g(\omega)$, for which the saturation factor is

$$\frac{1}{1 + \gamma^2 H_1^2 T_1 T_2}$$

using the definition of Eq. 3–61. Since the damping of the signal is proportional to $g(\omega)$, it follows that the center of an absorption peak will be more markedly affected than the periphery, and we frequently refer to this as *saturation broadening*. As this tends to obscure the magnetic resonance signal, and also various parts of a spectrum can be differently affected because of different relaxation times, we attempt to reduce the effects of saturation as much as possible. Since the saturation factor depends on the square of the H_1 field strength, we can generally eliminate the adverse effects by sufficient reduction of the H_1 field.

We might note in passing that there are occasions when we might wish to work at high H_1 fields. For example, our selection rule $\Delta m = \pm 1$ breaks down in the case of strong irradiation, for a full analysis of which the oscillating field H_1 must be included in the Hamiltonian. It turns out that *two-quantum transitions*, $\Delta m = \pm 2$, are allowed in this case. These transitions may be observed as weak satellite peaks, and are often useful in spectral analysis.

3-4 THE BLOCH EQUATIONS

Considerable insight into the macroscopic aspects of the magnetic resonance method can be gained by an examination of the so-called *Bloch equations*, which were introduced in an early attempt to account for NMR absorption. We proceed by noting, as previously mentioned, that the magnetization obeys the same equation of motion as the individual moments since they are simply related by

$$\mathbf{M} = \sum_{\substack{\text{unit} \\ \text{volume}}} \boldsymbol{\mu}_i$$

Hence we write (see Sec. 3–2, p. 44),

$$\frac{d\mathbf{M}}{dt} = -\gamma(\mathbf{H} \times \mathbf{M}) \tag{3–65}$$

We will as usual take $\mathbf{H_0}$ to be in the z-direction, and $\mathbf{H_1}$ to be in the xy-plane. With $\mathbf{H_1}$ rotating at an angular velocity ω, the components of the field $\mathbf{H} = \mathbf{H_0} + \mathbf{H_1}$ are,

$$H_x = H_1 \cos \omega t$$
$$H_y = -H_1 \sin \omega t$$
$$H_z = H_0$$

and Eq. 3–65 becomes

$$\frac{dM_x}{dt} = \gamma(M_z H_1 \sin \omega t + M_y H_0) \tag{3–65a}$$

$$\frac{dM_y}{dt} = \gamma(M_z H_1 \cos \omega t - M_x H_0) \tag{3–65b}$$

$$\frac{dM_z}{dt} = \gamma(-M_x H_1 \sin \omega t - M_y H_1 \cos \omega t) \tag{3–65c}$$

Relaxation also affects the magnetization, and must be incorporated into these equations. We have seen that the z-component of magnetization obeys an equation of the form

$$\frac{dM_z}{dt} = \frac{M_{z,\text{eq}} - M_z}{T_1} \tag{3–58}$$

for spin-lattice relaxation effects. $M_{z,\text{eq}}$ is the equilibrium value of M_z given by (see Eq. 3–27),

$$M_{z,\text{eq}} = \frac{N\mu^2}{kT} H_0 \tag{3–66}$$

for $F = \frac{1}{2}$. Thus the z-component equation becomes

$$\frac{dM_z}{dt} = \gamma(-M_x H_1 \sin \omega t - M_y H_1 \cos \omega t) - \frac{M_z - M_{z,\text{eq}}}{T_1} \tag{3–67}$$

which is the first of the Bloch equations. Because of the fact that spin-lattice relaxation affects only the M_z-component of magnetization directly, T_1 is sometimes referred to as the *longitudinal relaxation time*.

We need to consider the effect of spin-spin relaxation now. From Eq. 3–65, we know that, in the absence of relaxation, **M** would precess about the H_0 field direction if $H_1 \ll H_0$. However, the individual moments tend to get out of phase because of the spin-spin interactions. This loss of coherence causes a decay of the transverse, rotating components of the magnetization. The assumption is made that M_x and M_y decay by a first-order process, so that equations analogous to Eq. 3–58 can be written, where T_1 is replaced by T_2:

$$\frac{dM_x}{dt} = \frac{M_{x,\text{eq}} - M_x}{T_2} \qquad \frac{dM_y}{dt} = \frac{M_{y,\text{eq}} - M_y}{T_2}$$

In this case, time $t = \infty$ corresponds to a complete lack of coherence, so the vectorial sums of the transverse components vanish:

$$M_{x,\text{eq}} = \sum_{\substack{\text{unit} \\ \text{volume}}} \mu_{xi} = 0 \qquad M_{y,\text{eq}} = \sum_{\substack{\text{unit} \\ \text{volume}}} \mu_{yi} = 0$$

Thus, combining the effects of spin-spin relaxation with Eqs. 3–65a and b gives

$$\frac{dM_x}{dt} = \gamma(M_z H_1 \sin \omega t + M_y H_0) - \frac{M_x}{T_2} \qquad (3\text{–}68)$$

$$\frac{dM_y}{dt} = \gamma(M_z H_1 \cos \omega t - M_x H_0) - \frac{M_y}{T_2} \qquad (3\text{–}69)$$

which are the Bloch equations for the transverse components of magnetization. T_2 only appears in the differential equations for M_x and M_y, and it is therefore referred to at times as the *transverse relaxation time*. Because of the assumptions mentioned in the formulation of the Bloch equations, they must be regarded as phenomenological in nature and require an *a posteriori* justification.

The complete solution of the Bloch equations is difficult, and usually need not be considered since the essential features of magnetic resonance absorption can be illustrated by a steady-state solution. That is, we consider the H_0 and H_1 fields to have been applied for a sufficient period of time that M_z is constant, and M_x and M_y rotate with the H_1 field. The steady-state solution is most readily obtained by a transformation to a set of coordinates which rotates with the H_1 field. M_z will be unaffected, but M_x and M_y must be redefined in terms of the rotating frame. We define u to be the component of (M_x, M_y) which is *in phase* with the

H_1 field, and v to be the perpendicular component which is 90° *out of phase*. The transformation equations can be expressed as (see Fig. 3–7)

$$M_x = u \cos \omega t - v \sin \omega t \tag{3-70a}$$

$$M_y = -u \sin \omega t - v \cos \omega t \tag{3-70b}$$

In matrix form,

$$\begin{pmatrix} M_x \\ M_y \end{pmatrix} = \begin{pmatrix} \cos \omega t & -\sin \omega t \\ -\sin \omega t & -\cos \omega t \end{pmatrix} \begin{pmatrix} u \\ v \end{pmatrix}$$

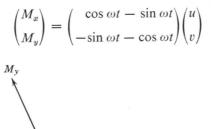

Fig. 3–7   In-phase and out-of-phase transverse components of the magnetization.

and by inversion of the transformation matrix, we obtain

$$u = M_x \cos \omega t - M_y \sin \omega t \tag{3-71a}$$

$$v = -M_x \sin \omega t - M_y \cos \omega t \tag{3-71b}$$

The Bloch equations can readily be written in terms of these newly defined coordinates with the use of the foregoing transformation equations. The result is

$$\frac{du}{dt} + \frac{u}{T_2} + (\omega_0 - \omega)v = 0 \tag{3-72a}$$

$$\frac{dv}{dt} + \frac{v}{T_2} - (\omega_0 - \omega)u + \gamma H_1 M_z = 0 \tag{3-72b}$$

$$\frac{dM_z}{dt} + \frac{M_z - M_{z,\text{eq}}}{T_1} - \gamma H_1 v = 0 \tag{3-72c}$$

The aforementioned steady-state conditions imply that u and v as well as M_z are constant. In this case we simply solve the equations

$$\frac{u}{T_2} + (\omega_0 - \omega)v = 0 \tag{3-73a}$$

$$\frac{v}{T_2} - (\omega_0 - \omega)u + \gamma H_1 M_z = 0 \tag{3-73b}$$

$$\frac{M_z - M_{z,\mathrm{eq}}}{T_1} - \gamma H_1 v = 0 \tag{3-73c}$$

The steady-state Bloch equations in a rotating frame can be readily solved by straightforward algebraic manipulation. We obtain

$$v = -M_{z,\mathrm{eq}} \frac{\gamma H_1 T_2}{L(\omega_0 - \omega)} \tag{3-74a}$$

$$u = M_{z,\mathrm{eq}} \frac{\gamma H_1 T_2{}^2(\omega_0 - \omega)}{L(\omega_0 - \omega)} \tag{3-74b}$$

$$M_z = M_{z,\mathrm{eq}} \frac{1 + T_2{}^2(\omega_0 - \omega)^2}{L(\omega_0 - \omega)} \tag{3-74c}$$

where $L(\omega_0 - \omega) = 1 + \gamma^2 H_1{}^2 T_1 T_2 + T_2{}^2(\omega_0 - \omega)^2$. These solutions can be transformed back to the fixed axes as follows: using Eq. 3-71, we obtain

$$-M_x \sin \omega t - M_y \cos \omega t = -M_{z,\mathrm{eq}} \frac{\gamma H_1 T_2}{L(\omega_0 - \omega)} \tag{3-75a}$$

$$M_x \cos \omega t - M_y \sin \omega t = M_{z,\mathrm{eq}} \frac{\gamma H_1 T_2{}^2(\omega_0 - \omega)}{L(\omega_0 - \omega)} \tag{3-75b}$$

Multiplying Eq. 3-75a by $\sin \omega t$ and Eq. 3-75b by $\cos \omega t$, and subtracting the first from the second, gives

$$M_x = M_{z,\mathrm{eq}} \frac{\gamma H_1 T_2{}^2(\omega_0 - \omega) \cos \omega t + \gamma H_1 T_2 \sin \omega t}{L(\omega_0 - \omega)}$$

Similarly, multiplication of Eq. 3-75a by $\cos \omega t$ and Eq. 3-75b by $\sin \omega t$, and adding the result, gives

$$M_y = M_{z,\mathrm{eq}} \frac{\gamma H_1 T_2 \cos \omega t - \gamma H_1 T_2{}^2(\omega_0 - \omega) \sin \omega t}{L(\omega_0 - \omega)}$$

To summarize, the steady-state solutions of Bloch's equations in the laboratory frame are

$$M_x = \frac{1}{2} M_{z,eq} \gamma T_2 \frac{T_2(\omega_0 - \omega)2H_1 \cos \omega t + 2H_1 \sin \omega t}{L(\omega_0 - \omega)} \quad (3\text{-}76a)$$

$$M_y = \frac{1}{2} M_{z,eq} \gamma T_2 \frac{2H_1 \cos \omega t - T_2(\omega_0 - \omega)2H_1 \sin \omega t}{L(\omega_0 - \omega)} \quad (3\text{-}76b)$$

$$M_z = M_{z,eq} \frac{1 + T_2^2(\omega_0 - \omega)^2}{L(\omega_0 - \omega)} \quad (3\text{-}76c)$$

We have written the equations in this form to emphasize the fact that we have derived them in terms of only one of the counterrotating components of a linear, oscillating field of magnitude $2H_1 \cos \omega t$ (see Sec. 3–2, p. 47). The component rotating in the same direction as the Larmor precession of the magnetization vector is of the same sign as ω_0, so $\omega_0 - \omega$ goes to zero at the resonance condition and the preceding equations describe the behavior of the magnetization. The effect of the other component is also included in Eqs. 3–76. In this case, since ω and ω_0 are of opposite sign, $\omega_0 - \omega$ remains a large number throughout the range through which the H_0 field is swept in a magnetic resonance experiment, so that its effect is negligible.

It is useful to think of the field $2H_1 \cos \omega t$ as producing an in-phase magnetization, $M' = 2\chi' H_1 \cos \omega t$, and an out-of-phase magnetization, $M'' = 2\chi'' H_1 \sin \omega t$. χ' and χ'' are known as the *Bloch susceptibilities*. Since M_x and M_y contain both in-phase and out-of-phase components, we define a complex susceptibility by

$$\chi = \chi' - i\chi'' \quad (3\text{-}77)$$

M_x is then taken to be the real component of the magnetization,

$$M_x = \text{Re}\,(\chi 2H_1 e^{i\omega t})$$

from which it follows that

$$M_x = \chi' 2H_1 \cos \omega t + \chi'' 2H_1 \sin \omega t$$

Comparing this with Eq. 3–76a, we get

$$\chi' = \frac{1}{2} \chi_{eq} \omega_0 \frac{T_2^2(\omega_0 - \omega)}{L(\omega_0 - \omega)} \quad (3\text{-}78a)$$

and

$$\chi'' = \frac{1}{2} \chi_{eq} \omega_0 \frac{T_2}{L(\omega_0 - \omega)} \quad (3\text{-}78b)$$

χ_{eq} is the equilibrium static susceptibility defined for the spin $\frac{1}{2}$ case by (see Eq. 3–66)

$$\chi_{eq} = \frac{M_{z,eq}}{H_0} = \frac{N\mu^2}{kT} \tag{3-79}$$

Let us now turn to a consideration of the power absorbed by the sample from the H_1 field. The mean rate of energy absorption per unit volume of sample, A, is given by

$$A = H_x \overline{\frac{dM_x}{dt}}$$

$$= \frac{2M_{z,eq}\gamma T_2 \omega H_1^2}{L(\omega_0 - \omega)} \overline{\left[\cos^2 \omega t - T_2(\omega_0 - \omega)^2 \sin \omega t \cos \omega t \right]} \tag{3-80}$$

It can be readily shown that

$$\overline{\cos^2 \omega t} = \tfrac{1}{2} \qquad \text{and} \qquad \overline{\sin \omega t \cos \omega t} = 0$$

so we have

$$A = \frac{\gamma \omega H_1^2 M_{z,eq} T_2}{1 + T_2^2(\omega_0 - \omega)^2 + \gamma^2 H_1^2 T_1 T_2} \tag{3-81}$$

This obviously goes through a maximum at $\omega = \omega_0$, as would be expected. Comparing Eq. 3–81 with Eq. 3–78b, we see that the power absorption is readily expressed in terms of the out-of-phase Bloch susceptibility. We find that

$$A = 2\omega H_1^2 \chi'' \tag{3-82}$$

We can now derive an expression for the line-shape function $g(\omega)$, which was introduced in Sec. 3–2, p. 52. We have seen that the population change caused by induced transitions between the $-\frac{1}{2}$ and $+\frac{1}{2}$ states is (Sec. 3–3, p. 59)

$$Pn = \tfrac{1}{4}\gamma^2 H_1^2 g(\omega)(n_+ - n_-)$$

$$= \frac{1}{4}\gamma^2 H_1^2 g(\omega)\left[\frac{N}{2}\left(1 + \frac{\mu H_0}{kT_s}\right) - \frac{N}{2}\left(1 - \frac{\mu H_0}{kT_s}\right) \right]$$

$$= \frac{1}{4}\gamma^2 H_1^2 g(\omega) \frac{N\mu H_0}{kT_s}$$

Here we have taken explicit account of the fact that the spin temperature may be different from the lattice temperature. Since each of the net upward transitions requires the absorption of a quantum of energy $h\nu$, we write,

$$A = \frac{1}{4}\gamma^2 H_1^2 g(\omega) \frac{N\mu H_0}{kT_s} h\nu \tag{3-83}$$

Equating Eq. 3–83 and Eq. 3–82, we find that

$$g(\omega) = \frac{8\omega k T_s}{\gamma^2 N \mu H_0 h \nu} \chi'' \tag{3-84}$$

Near resonance, we can write $h\nu \approx h\nu_0 = 2\mu H_0$ and $\omega \approx \omega_0$. This gives

$$g(\omega) = \frac{4\omega_0 k T_s}{\gamma^2 N \mu^2 H_0^2} \chi'' = \frac{4\chi''}{\omega_0 \chi_s} \tag{3-85}$$

where

$$\chi_s = \frac{N\mu^2}{k T_s} \tag{3-86}$$

is the static susceptibility at the spin temperature T_s. Using Eq. 3–52, it is obvious that

$$\frac{n_{eq}}{n} = \frac{(n_+ - n_-)_{eq}}{n_+ - n_-} = \frac{N(\mu H_0/kT)}{N(\mu H_0/k T_s)} = \frac{T_s}{T}$$

However, we have seen that (Sec. 3–3, p. 60)

$$\frac{n}{n_{eq}} = \frac{1}{1 + \frac{1}{2}\gamma^2 H_1^2 T_1 g(\omega)} \equiv Z$$

Thus, $T_s = T/Z$, and

$$\chi_s = \frac{N\mu^2 Z}{kT} = \chi_{eq} Z$$

We finally obtain

$$g(\omega) = \frac{4}{Z\omega_0 \chi_{eq}} \chi'' \tag{3-87}$$

and note that the line-shape function is proportional to the Bloch susceptibility χ''.

If we now assume that H_1 is sufficiently small so that $\gamma^2 H_1^2 T_1 T_2 \ll 1$, then $Z = 1$ and

$$g(\omega) = \frac{2T_2}{1 + T_2^2(\omega_0 - \omega)^2}$$

A line-shape function of this form is known as a Lorentzian curve, and it is of the same form as χ'', which is shown in Fig. 3–8a, b. It will be observed that $g(\omega)$ is a maximum at $\omega = \omega_0$, for which

$$[g(\omega)]_{max} = 2T_2$$

This is the justification for writing Eq. 3–61.

By suitable adjustment of the experimental conditions, we can observe either the *absorption mode* which is related to χ'' (Fig. 3–8a), or the *dispersion mode* which is related to χ' (Fig. 3–8b). These are alternatively referred to as the *v-mode* signal and the *u-mode* signal respectively. They are, of course, not independent, but are related to one another through

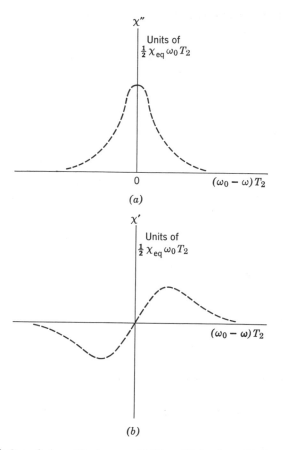

Fig. 3–8   (*a*) Out-of-phase Bloch susceptibility;   (*b*) in-phase Bloch susceptibility.

the particular form of the Bloch equations. This is but a special case of the Kramers-Kronig relations which are discussed by Andrew (Ref. 2).

The Lorentzian line shape we have derived here occurs in numerous physical theories involving damped harmonic oscillation, and it arises because of the assumption of an exponential decay caused by relaxation. More general line shapes are found experimentally. They can be treated quantum-mechanically by using a perturbation-theory approach which involves no assumption of a particular form for $g(\omega)$.

3-5   EXCHANGE PHENOMENA

If magnetic resonance occurred at a single, fixed frequency in a given magnetic field, it would be of little interest to the chemist. It is because of the fact that resonance occurs at several frequencies that useful structural information can be obtained. In general, the environmental influences within a given chemical species are sufficient to produce several magnetic resonance lines, collectively referred to as the spectrum. We can frequently regard the spectrum as being composed of several separate resonances, each of which is subject to the same sort of treatment as that outlined in the last section for a single resonance.

It sometimes happens that a given magnetic moment is free to change physically from one environment to another with sufficient rapidity that the foregoing analysis is no longer valid. Such a situation is referred to as *exchange*, and it can result from such various effects as internal rotations in molecules, tautomerism, and intermolecular reactions. We will investigate here the effect of exchange on line shapes.

It is useful to define a complex moment G by (see Eq. 3–77)

$$G = u + iv \tag{3–88}$$

where u and v are the components of M_x and M_y which are in phase and out of phase with the H_1 field, as previously defined. Differentiation of Eq. 3–88 gives

$$\frac{dG}{dt} = \frac{du}{dt} + i\frac{dv}{dt}$$

Using this, the first two Bloch equations (Eqs. 3–72a and b) can be written as the single complex equation,

$$\frac{dG}{dt} + \frac{G}{T_2} - i(\omega_0 - \omega)G = -i\gamma H_1 M_{z,\text{eq}} \tag{3–89}$$

where it has been assumed that H_1 is sufficiently small that $M_z \approx M_{z,\text{eq}}$.

We now consider two different resonances, which correspond to the Larmor frequencies ω_A and ω_B. In the absence of exchange, these two systems obey separate Bloch equations of the form

$$\frac{dG_A}{dt} + \alpha_A G_A = -i\gamma H_1 M_{z,\text{eq}_A} \tag{3–90a}$$

$$\frac{dG_B}{dt} + \alpha_B G_B = -i\gamma H_1 M_{z,\text{eq}_B} \tag{3–90b}$$

where

$$\alpha_A = \frac{1}{T_{2_A}} - i(\omega_A - \omega) \tag{3-91a}$$

$$\alpha_B = \frac{1}{T_{2_B}} - i(\omega_B - \omega) \tag{3-91b}$$

If we now assume an exchange to take place, there will be a transfer of magnetization between the A system and the B system. We define the mean lifetime of a given magnetic moment in the A system to be τ_A, with a similar definition for τ_B. The population numbers are obviously

$$p_A = \frac{\tau_A}{\tau_A + \tau_B} \quad \text{and} \quad p_B = \frac{\tau_B}{\tau_A + \tau_B}$$

With transitions from the B to the A system, there is a transfer of magnetization, G_B/τ_B. An amount G_A/τ_A is likewise transferred from the A system to the B system. We thus write in place of the Bloch equations (Eqs. 3–90),

$$\frac{dG_A}{dt} + \alpha_A G_A = -i\gamma H_1 M_{z,eq_A} + \frac{G_B}{\tau_B} - \frac{G_A}{\tau_A} \tag{3-92a}$$

$$\frac{dG_B}{dt} + \alpha_B G_B = -i\gamma H_1 M_{z,eq_B} + \frac{G_A}{\tau_A} - \frac{G_B}{\tau_B} \tag{3-92b}$$

Let us now assume that we sweep through resonance slowly enough that the magnetization follows the steady-state conditions. We call this *slow passage*, for which, in this case,

$$\frac{dG_A}{dt} = \frac{dG_B}{dt} = 0$$

Taking note of the fact that

$$M_{z,eq_A} = p_A M_{z,eq} \quad \text{and} \quad M_{z,eq_B} = p_B M_{z,eq}$$

the steady-state solutions can be written,

$$G_A = -i\gamma H_1 M_{z,eq} \frac{\tau_A(1 + p_A\alpha_B\tau_B)}{(1 + \alpha_A\tau_A)(1 + \alpha_B\tau_B) - 1}$$

$$G_B = -i\gamma H_1 M_{z,eq} \frac{\tau_B(1 + p_B\alpha_A\tau_A)}{(1 + \alpha_A\tau_A)(1 + \alpha_B\tau_B) - 1}$$

and

$$G = G_A + G_B = -i\gamma H_1 M_{z,eq} \frac{\tau_A + \tau_B + \tau_A\tau_B(\alpha_B p_A + \alpha_A p_B)}{(1 + \alpha_A\tau_A)(1 + \alpha_B\tau_B) - 1} \tag{3-93}$$

The complete solution of this equation for u and v is quite complicated, so we will examine approximate solutions in a few special cases.

By *slow exchange*, we mean that

$$\tau_A, \tau_B \gg \frac{1}{\omega_A - \omega_B}$$

In this case, there will be two more or less unperturbed resonances, as can be seen as follows: Near the frequency ω_A, the v-mode signal can be attributed mainly to G_A. Setting $G_B = 0$ in Eq. 3-92a and solving the resulting equation for slow-passage conditions gives

$$G \approx G_A = \frac{-i\gamma H_1 p_A M_{z,eq} \tau_A}{1 + \alpha_A \tau_A}$$

This is, of course, equal to $u + iv$, so the individual dispersion and absorption modes can be found by equating real and imaginary parts. We obtain for the absorption mode,

$$v = \frac{-\gamma H_1 p_A M_{z,eq}[\tau_A T_{2_A}/(T_{2_A} + \tau_A)]}{1 + [T_{2_A}^2 \tau_A^2/(T_{2_A} + \tau_A)^2](\omega_A - \omega)^2} \tag{3-94}$$

This is again a Lorentzian curve, and it differs in form from the v-mode signal derived in Sec. 3-4 only in that it is characterized by a width

$$\frac{1}{T_{2_A}'} = \frac{1}{T_{2_A}} + \frac{1}{\tau_A}$$

rather than

$$\frac{1}{T_{2_A}}$$

Of course there is also a signal centered at ω_B with width,

$$\frac{1}{T_{2_B}'} = \frac{1}{T_{2_B}} + \frac{1}{\tau_B}$$

Now in the limit of *fast exchange*, τ_A and τ_B are very small. In this case, quadratic terms in τ_A and τ_B can be neglected in Eq. 3-93, and we obtain

$$G \approx -i\gamma H_1 M_{z,eq} \frac{\tau_A + \tau_B}{\alpha_A \tau_A + \alpha_B \tau_B} = -i\gamma H_1 M_{z,eq} \frac{1}{p_A \alpha_A + p_B \alpha_B}$$

We again solve for the u and v modes by equating real and imaginary parts of this expression for G. Noting that $p_A + p_B = 1$, we obtain

$$v = \frac{-i\gamma H_1 M_{z,eq}(p_A/T_{2_A} + p_B/T_{2_B})^{-1}}{1 + (p_A/T_{2_A} + p_B/T_{2_B})^{-2}(p_A \omega_A + p_B \omega_B - \omega)^2} \tag{3-95}$$

This is the equation for a Lorentzian curve centered at

$$p_A \omega_A + p_B \omega_B$$

whose width is

$$\frac{1}{T_2'} = \frac{p_A}{T_{2_A}} + \frac{p_B}{T_{2_B}}$$

As we have already noted, the intermediate cases are difficult to solve in general. Gutowsky and Holm have given a solution for the case in

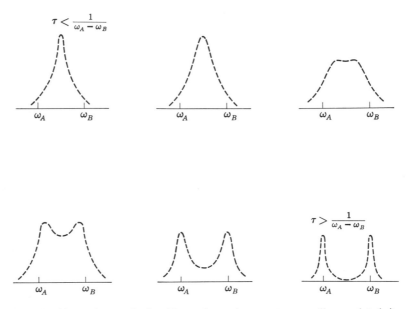

Fig. 3–9   Absorption-mode signal for exchange between two equally populated sites.

which T_{2_A} and T_{2_B} are equal. For $\tau_A = \tau_B \equiv \tau$, the v mode is found to be

$$v = -\tfrac{1}{4}\gamma H_1 M_{z,\text{eq}} \frac{\tau(\omega_A - \omega_B)^2}{[\tfrac{1}{2}(\omega_A + \omega_B) - \omega]^2 + \tau^2(\omega_A - \omega)^2(\omega_B - \omega)^2} \quad (3\text{–}96)$$

in the limit of very large transverse relaxation times. With $\tau_A = \tau_B$, it is obvious that $p_A = p_B = \frac{1}{2}$, so that the foregoing solution applies to the case of two equal signals whose width in the absence of exchange is very small compared to the separation between them. The behavior in the intermediate exchange region is illustrated in Fig. 3–9.

SUPPLEMENTARY READING

1. J. H. Van Vleck, *Electric and Magnetic Susceptibilities*, Oxford University Press, New York, 1932.
2. E. R. Andrew, *Nuclear Magnetic Resonance*, Cambridge University Press, New York, 1958.
3. J. A. Pople, W. G. Schneider, and H. J. Bernstein, *High-Resolution Nuclear Magnetic Resonance*, McGraw-Hill Book Company, New York, 1959.
4. R. E. Richards, Nuclear Magnetic Resonance, in *Advances in Spectroscopy*, H. W. Thompson (Ed.), Interscience Publishers, New York, Vol. II, 1961.
5. G. E. Pake, *Paramagnetic Resonance*, W. A. Benjamin, New York, 1962.
6. A. Abragam, *The Principles of Nuclear Magnetism*, Oxford University Press, New York, 1961.
7. C. P. Slichter, *Principles of Magnetic Resonance*, Harper & Row, New York, 1963.
8. E. M. Purcell, H. C. Torrey, and R. V. Pound, "Resonance Absorption by Nuclear Magnetic Moments in a Solid," *Phys. Rev.*, **69,** 37 (1946).
9. R. C. Tolman, *The Principles of Statistical Mechanics*, Oxford University Press, New York, 1938.

4

Nuclear Magnetic Resonance

4–1 EXPERIMENTAL METHODS

The essential features of a nuclear magnetic resonance (NMR) spectrometer can be readily inferred from our previous discussions. We obviously need a strong magnetic field H_0 which serves the purpose of polarizing the nuclear moments of the sample, together with a linear, oscillating H_1 field perpendicular to it. The power absorption from the H_1 field can serve as the means of detection.

It is useful to begin by mentioning the magnitude of the magnetic-field strengths involved, as well as the H_1 field frequencies. They are related by the Larmor condition,

$$\nu_0 = \frac{\gamma H_0}{2\pi} \tag{4–1}$$

and cannot be regarded as independent. Using information contained in Table 2–1 and relationships given in Chap. 2, we can readily construct Table 4–1, which gives the frequencies and field strengths at which NMR is observed for several common nuclei. It will be seen that H_1 is in the radio-frequency (r-f) range for H_0 fields of the order of 10^4 gauss. As we shall see later, there are advantages to working at higher field strengths, but there are limits on how far we can go and still have sufficient field homogeneity to obtain useful data.

A block diagram of a simple NMR spectrometer is shown in Fig. 4–1. The blocks labeled N and S represent the poles of the large H_0 magnet, which is usually an electromagnet operated through a stabilized power supply. Permanent magnets have often been used in broad-line or solid-state work, but until recently they did not have sufficient homogeneity at large enough field strengths to be very useful for high-resolution work. Quite recently, superconducting solenoids operating at liquid helium temperatures have also been used. Stability is no problem in this case, and very large field strengths are attainable, although the continuous consumption of liquid helium constitutes a rather serious practical limitation.

With frequency and field strength related through Eq. 4–1, we can obviously vary either one of them to fulfill the resonance condition, as we have already noted. In practice it is convenient to use a fixed-frequency r-f source, since crystal-controlled oscillators whose stability is of the order of 1 part in 10^9 are available. Nuclear magnetic resonance absorption occurs over a relatively narrow range of field strengths, at fixed

Table 4–1 *NMR Field Strengths and Frequencies of Some Common Nuclei**

Isotope	5 Mc/sec	20 Mc/sec	60 Mc/sec	100 Mc/sec
H^1	1,174	4,697	14,092	23,487
H^2	7,650	30,600	91,800	153,000
Li^7	3,022	12,087	36,260	60,434
B^{11}	3,660	14,641	43,924	73,206
C^{13}	4,671	18,683	56,049	93,414
N^{14}	16,260	65,020	195,100	325,000
O^{17}	9,566	38,260	114,800	191,300
F^{19}	1,248	4,993	14,979	24,966
Na^{23}	4,440	17,759	53,276	88,794
Al^{27}	4,507	18,028	54,083	90,139
Si^{29}	5,910	23,640	70,920	118,200
P^{31}	2,901	11,604	34,813	58,021
Cl^{35}	11,980	47,940	143,800	239,700
Cl^{37}	14,400	57,600	172,800	288,000
Br^{79}	4,687	18,749	56,248	93,747
Br^{81}	4,349	17,394	52,183	86,972
I^{127}	5,869	23,480	70,430	117,400

* In gauss.

frequency, and an auxiliary set of sweep coils supplied by a d-c source can be used to vary the field strength throughout the range of resonance. These coils, together with additional "shim" coils which are used to make minor corrections for field inhomogeneity are located in the sample holder, which is referred to as the *probe* in NMR spectroscopy.

The H_1 oscillating field is provided by the r-f current flow through a coil perpendicular to H_0 surrounding the sample at s. A large resistor R is used in the r-f circuit to ensure a somewhat constant current, and the capacitor C is tuned to achieve a balance. As the d-c sweep current is varied and the resonance condition is fulfilled, there is an absorption of power from the coil at s. This unbalances the r-f bridge circuit and a voltage drop across the sample coil is observed. This voltage drop is detected as the NMR signal following amplification.

An enhancement of the sensitivity can be achieved by modulation of the H_0 field using a low-frequency a-c oscillation. This is accomplished through an additional coil in the probe, as indicated in Fig. 4–1. This modulation about the resonant field strength causes the sample to pass in and out of resonance twice in each cycle. The signal can then be displayed on an oscilloscope or graphically recorded following phase-sensitive detection.

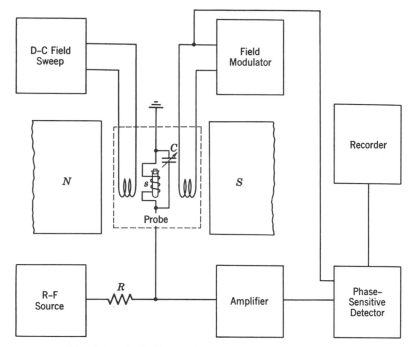

Fig. 4–1   Block diagram for a simple NMR spectrometer.

There is a fundamental difficulty with the experimental arrangement we have described here. The amplifier receives the entire voltage applied across s, and is thus limited by the fact that the NMR signal constitutes only a small voltage change. There are several ways of avoiding this difficulty. One method is the use of an additional coil to pick up an induced signal. This is the nuclear-induction method to be described in the following subsection. A second method uses a r-f bridge to balance the input so that *only* the signal resulting from an unbalance is detected. Figure 4–2 shows a circuit which does this. It operates as follows: The signal arriving at the amplifier is a composite of two signals which have traversed different branches of the circuit. The first of these has passed through the capacitors C_1 and C_2. Since there is a 180° phase change at each capacitor for the r-f current, it follows that this first signal is approximately in phase with the input current, although minor phase shifts can be made by the tuning of C_4. The other signal passes through a single capacitor C_3, and is thus 180° out of phase with the input. There is an effective voltage divider in this branch of the circuit, however, so that amplitude adjustments in the second signal can be made by tuning the capacitor C_5. Thus, tuning with respect to both phase and amplitude

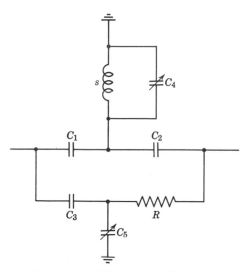

Fig. 4–2   Radio-frequency bridge circuit.

are possible by varying C_4 and C_5 respectively. With the bridge tuned to eliminate effectively the input signal, the voltage drop at resonance represents a large, relative change.

It will be recalled that a NMR signal is composed of so-called u and v modes which are 90° out of phase with one another. The u mode can be detected by unbalancing the r-f bridge with respect to phase. Since the u mode is in phase with the applied r-f field, this unbalance will be markedly affected by the u mode at the resonance condition, whereas the v mode will contribute very little to the observed signal. Similarly, the bridge can be unbalanced with respect to amplitude by proper tuning of C_5. In this case the v mode contributes the predominate effect, and the absorption rather than the dispersion signal will be observed.

Another technique frequently used to enhance the sensitivity, particularly where broad resonance lines are being observed, is to employ an audio-frequency (a-f) modulation of the magnetic field. If the amplitude

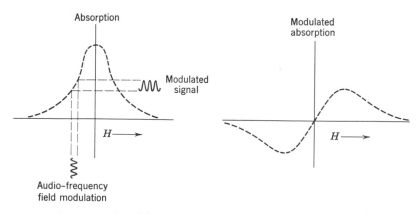

Fig. 4–3   Effect of field modulation on an absorption-mode signal.

of the modulation is small with respect to the line width, the modulated signal will be proportional to the slope of the NMR signal. This is illustrated in Fig. 4–3 for the v-mode signal. Using phase-sensitive detection of the modulated signal, the first derivative of the absorption peak is detected, which is also shown in Fig. 4–3.

Nuclear Induction

Present-day NMR spectrometers frequently use separate coils for excitation and detection of nuclear resonances. These coils are mutually perpendicular to each other as well as to the polarizing field, and hence this is sometimes spoken of as a crossed-coil system (see Fig. 4–4). This perpendicular arrangement insures that no signal will be induced directly in the receiving coil. However, nuclei in the sample which have been excited to an upper spin state emit energy as they fall back to lower levels, and through this mechanism a signal is induced in the receiving coil at resonance. This is called a *nuclear-induction* signal, and it can be amplified and detected in the same manner as previously described.

The idealized perpendicularity of the transmitting and receiving coils is difficult to achieve in practice. We actually obtain a certain degree of capacitive coupling owing to incomplete orthogonality. To avoid this difficulty, *paddles* are used in the probe to steer the flux between the two coils so that direct coupling is eliminated. One of these paddles is constructed of conducting material such as copper. The conducting paddle acts as a double capacitor, and it controls induced voltages in the receiving coil which are in phase with the transmitting coil. The second paddle is made of an insulating material, and it controls induced voltages in the receiving coil which are approximately 180° out of phase with the transmitting coil. A leakage can be induced by detuning either of these paddles, and whether we detect the u-mode or v-mode signal in the receiving coil depends on the manner in which the probe is detuned. Leakage induced by detuning with respect to the conducting paddle carries the u-mode signal, whereas the v-mode signal can be observed by

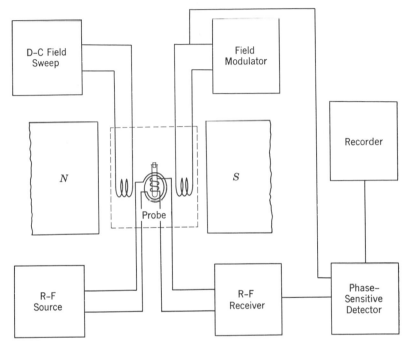

Fig. 4–4   Block diagram for a crossed-coil NMR spectrometer.

detuning with the insulating paddle. The analogy between this and the unbalancing of a r-f bridge in phase and amplitude as described in the last section is obvious.

Quantitatively, the voltage which is induced in the receiver coil along the y-axis, with the transmitter coil along the x-axis, is given by

$$V = -K \frac{dM_y}{dt} \qquad (4\text{-}2)$$

where K is a constant which depends on the sample and on the coil geometry. In terms of the Bloch susceptibilities (see Sec. 3–4),

$$M_y = 2H_1(\chi'' \cos \omega t - \chi' \sin \omega t)$$

so we obtain,

$$V = 2K\omega H_1(\chi'' \sin \omega t + \chi' \cos \omega t) \tag{4-3}$$

Thus, the u-mode signal is proportional to $\omega H_1 \chi'$, or

$$u \propto \frac{\omega \chi_0 H_0 \gamma H_1 T_2^2(\omega_0 - \omega)}{1 + T_2^2(\omega_0 - \omega)^2 + \gamma^2 H_1^2 T_1 T_2} \tag{4-4}$$

and the v-mode signal is proportional to $\omega H_1 \chi''$, or

$$v \propto \frac{\omega \chi_0 H_0 \gamma H_1 T_2}{1 + T_2^2(\omega_0 - \omega)^2 + \gamma^2 H_1^2 T_1 T_2} \tag{4-5}$$

We frequently use peak intensities in the analysis of NMR spectra, although it is the peak areas which are proportional to the number of nuclei making a given transition between energy states. We can investigate the validity of such an approximation by using the foregoing expressions. If we observe the absorption-mode signal, we find the area by integration of Eq. 4–5 to be

$$A \propto \frac{\chi_0 H_1}{(1 + \gamma^2 H_1^2 T_1 T_2)^{1/2}} \tag{4-6}$$

whereas the corresponding peak height is

$$S \propto \frac{\chi_0 H_1 T_2}{1 + \gamma^2 H_1^2 T_1 T_2} \tag{4-7}$$

We see that peak-height comparisons are valid only if H_1 is sufficiently small so that $\gamma^2 H_1^2 T_1 T_2 \ll 1$. It is furthermore required that the transverse-relaxation times be equivalent.

Experiments in Pulsed R-F Fields

If the strength of the H_0 magnetic field is varied sufficiently slowly, at fixed frequency, so that the steady-state solution to Bloch's equations is valid, we speak of *slow-passage* conditions. With H_1 sufficiently small so that saturation effects can be neglected, the component of **M** in the xy-plane, known as $\mathbf{M}_{xy}$, traces out a circle in the rotating frame which passes through the origin (Fig. 4–5). This can be seen by an inspection of the Eqs. 3–74a and b. With H_0 far below the resonance value, u and v are both zero and **M** is parallel to $\mathbf{H}_0$. As ω approaches ω_0, $\mathbf{M}_{xy}$ grows in magnitude, until at $\omega = \omega_0$ it comes to a point labeled P on the circle. It subsequently decreases back to zero as H_0 increases past the resonant value. During this process, the magnetization vector is tipped away from the $\mathbf{H}_0$ field direction, following which it returns to its equilibrium position along $\mathbf{H}_0$.

Now let us assume that we apply a short r-f pulse of the appropriate resonance frequency. This will have the effect of tipping the magnetization away from the H_0 field direction. Thus, when the pulse is terminated, the magnetization vector is left in a nonequilibrium orientation, and it will undergo a subsequent precessional motion about $\mathbf{H_0}$. This precession will be at the Larmor frequency, and it will continue until $\mathbf{M}_{xy}$ decays to

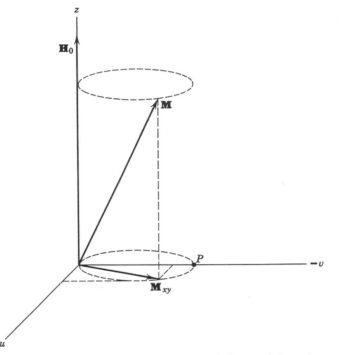

Fig. 4–5   Behavior of the magnetization vector as H_0 is increased through resonance.

zero by transverse-relaxation effects. In a perfectly homogeneous field, the rate of decay of the v-mode signal is thus given by e^{-t/T_2}. The decaying signal following a single r-f pulse is known as *free-induction decay*.

Field inhomogeneity makes the decay of $\mathbf{M}_{xy}$ more rapid than would be caused by relaxation effects alone. The effect of the field inhomogeneity is to give varying Larmor frequencies to nuclei which are located in different parts of the sample. Following a r-f pulse, the magnetization vector has been tipped away from the z-direction and is rotating out of phase with H_1. If we define x^* and y^* to be coordinates in a frame of reference which is rotating at the *mean* Larmor frequency, with x^* in phase with H_1, then $\mathbf{M}_{xy}$ is in the H_0y^*-plane following the r-f pulse.

$\mathbf{M}_{xy}$ continues to precess about $\mathbf{H}_0$, but the decay of the perpendicular component is more rapid now because of the difference in the Larmor frequencies. Some nuclei precess faster than the mean, and some more slowly than the mean, so there is a "fanning out" of the perpendicular component of $\mathbf{M}$ as viewed in the rotating frame. This effect enhances the decay of $\mathbf{M}_{xy}$, as illustrated in Fig. 4–6. If it is assumed that the field inhomogeneity gives rise to a Larmor-frequency distribution which

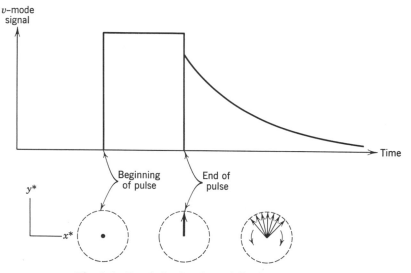

Fig. 4–6   Free-induction decay following an r-f pulse.

can be approximated by a Lorentzian-type curve, it can be readily shown that the signal decays with a characteristic time constant T_m, where

$$\frac{1}{T_m} = \frac{1}{T_2} + \frac{1}{T_2^*}$$

T_2^* is a constant analogous to T_2 which characterizes the width of the frequency distribution due to field inhomogeneity. By comparative studies in a given field where T_2^* can be regarded as constant, it is possible to determine relative values of T_2 from the measured values of T_m.

Unless the transverse-relaxation time happens to be very short, the free-induction decay is usually predominated by field inhomogeneity rather than by relaxation. There is an alternative method of determining T_2 which can be used in this case, known as the method of *spin echoes*. A very intense H_1 field is used, and the pulse is made for a sufficiently short period of time that relaxation effects can be neglected *during* the pulse. Under these conditions, **M** smoothly rotates away from the $\mathbf{H_0}$ direction with an angular velocity γH_1. If the time of the pulse, t_w, is chosen so that

$$\gamma H_1 t_w = \frac{\pi}{2}$$

then **M** will be rotated exactly to the xy-plane, and we speak of a *90° pulse*. Similarly, application of a pulse for a time $2t_w$ with the same H_1

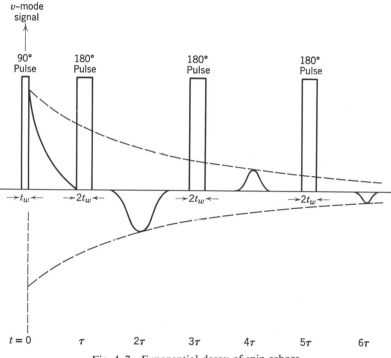

Fig. 4–7 Exponential decay of spin echoes.

field strength will completely reverse the orientation of **M**, and this is known as a *180° pulse*.

In the spin-echo method, we begin by applying a 90° pulse, followed by a 180° pulse at a later time τ. During the intervening time, free-induction decay has taken place, and the individual spin vectors have fanned out in the x^*y^*-plane from the y^*-direction. The 180° pulse rotates each of the individual spin vectors by 180°, however, so that they begin to reverse their motion following the second pulse and, at a time 2τ, they will be regrouped in the negative y^*-direction. Hence, there results a signal that is negative with respect to the original v-mode signal, which is known as the spin echo. It is reduced in intensity by an amount depending on relaxation, because the one effect of field inhomogeneity is the fanning of the moments, and this has been reversed by the 180° pulse. We can continue this process, applying 180° pulses at $\tau, 3\tau, 5\tau, \ldots$, with resulting spin echoes at $2\tau, 4\tau, 6\tau, \ldots$. These echoes will fall on an exponential curve of the form $e^{-2\tau/T_2}$, which allows T_2 to be determined (see Fig. 4–7).

This analysis breaks down if the moments move about significantly in an inhomogeneous field owing to diffusion, since the Larmor frequency for a given magnetic moment will no longer be constant. The amplitude of the spin echoes will be affected by this motion and, by noting this effect, the coefficients of self-diffusion can be determined by purposely making the field very inhomogeneous.

4–2 BROAD-LINE NMR

There is a magnetic field associated with each magnetic moment in a given sample. Each of the moments is affected by the field of all the others, so that the effective field at a given nuclear site is not H_0 but

$$H = H_0 + H_{\text{local}} \tag{4–8}$$

If the molecules of the sample are free to tumble about rapidly, as in the liquid and gaseous states, these local-field effects are averaged out and no direct interaction between the nuclear moments is observed. In the solid state, however, the nuclear moments are fixed, and hence the resonance frequency varies with position within the sample. The local fields, owing to these interacting moments, tend to broaden out the magnetic resonance absorption over a considerable range. Hence we use the term, *broad-line NMR*, although *solid-state NMR* would do as well.

Let us for simplicity assume that we have pairs of interacting nuclei of spin $I = \frac{1}{2}$ in the sample, with these pairs widely enough separated from other such pairs that each can be considered independently. The classical interaction energy of two magnetic dipoles μ_1 and μ_2, which are separated by a distance r, is

$$\frac{\mu_1 \cdot \mu_2}{r^3} - \frac{3(\mu_1 \cdot r)(\mu_2 \cdot r)}{r^5}$$

Writing $\mu = \gamma_N \hbar I$ (Eq. 2–44), and constructing the Hamiltonian operator, gives

$$\hat{H}_{12} = \gamma_N{}^2 \hbar^2 \left[\frac{\hat{I}_1 \cdot \hat{I}_2}{r^3} - \frac{3(\hat{I}_1 \cdot r)(\hat{I}_2 \cdot r)}{r^5} \right] \tag{4–9}$$

We define a unit vector $\mathbf{n} = \mathbf{r}/r$, in which case Eq. 4–9 becomes

$$\hat{H}_{12} = \frac{\gamma_N^2 \hbar^2}{r^3} [\hat{\mathbf{I}}_1 \cdot \hat{\mathbf{I}}_2 - 3(\hat{\mathbf{I}}_1 \cdot \mathbf{n})(\hat{\mathbf{I}}_2 \cdot \mathbf{n})] \qquad (4\text{–}10)$$

$\mathbf{n}$ can be written in terms of the orthogonal set of unit vectors, $\mathbf{i}$, $\mathbf{j}$, and $\mathbf{k}$, defining the directions x, y, and z respectively, as

$$\mathbf{n} = n_1\mathbf{i} + n_2\mathbf{j} + n_3\mathbf{k} \qquad (4\text{–}11)$$

where n_1, n_2, and n_3 are the direction cosines. Using the usual definition of spherical polar coordinates,

$$n_1 = \sin\theta\cos\phi \qquad n_2 = \sin\theta\sin\phi \qquad n_3 = \cos\theta \qquad (4\text{–}12)$$

Writing $\hat{\mathbf{I}}_1$ and $\hat{\mathbf{I}}_2$ also in terms of unit vectors,

$$\hat{\mathbf{I}}_1 = \hat{I}_{x_1}\mathbf{i} + \hat{I}_{y_1}\mathbf{j} + \hat{I}_{z_1}\mathbf{k} \qquad \hat{\mathbf{I}}_2 = \hat{I}_{x_2}\mathbf{i} + \hat{I}_{y_2}\mathbf{j} + \hat{I}_{z_2}\mathbf{k}$$

$\hat{H}_{12}$ can be written in the form,

$$\hat{H}_{12} = \frac{\gamma_N^2 \hbar^2}{r^3} (A + B + C + D + E + F) \qquad (4\text{–}13)$$

where the various angular dependent terms have been collected as follows:

$$A = \hat{I}_{z_1}\hat{I}_{z_2}(1 - 3\cos^2\theta) \qquad (4\text{–}14a)$$

$$B = -\tfrac{1}{4}\hat{I}_{-_1}\hat{I}_{+_2}\hat{I}_{+_1}\hat{I}_{-_2}(1 - 3\cos^2\theta) \qquad (4\text{–}14b)$$

$$C = -\tfrac{3}{2}(\hat{I}_{+_1}\hat{I}_{z_2} + \hat{I}_{+_2}\hat{I}_{z_1})\sin\theta\cos\theta\,e^{-i\phi} \qquad (4\text{–}14c)$$

$$D = -\tfrac{3}{2}(\hat{I}_{-_1}\hat{I}_{z_2} + \hat{I}_{-_2}\hat{I}_{z_1})\sin\theta\cos\theta\,e^{i\phi} \qquad (4\text{–}14d)$$

$$E = -\tfrac{3}{4}\hat{I}_{+_1}\hat{I}_{+_2}\sin^2\theta\,e^{-2i\phi} \qquad (4\text{–}14e)$$

$$F = -\tfrac{3}{4}\hat{I}_{-_1}\hat{I}_{-_2}\sin^2\theta\,e^{2i\phi} \qquad (4\text{–}14f)$$

Here we have used our previous definition of raising and lowering operators (Eq. 2–36), as well as the identities,

$$\cos\phi = \tfrac{1}{2}(e^{i\phi} + e^{-i\phi}) \qquad \text{and} \qquad \sin\phi = \frac{1}{2i}(e^{i\phi} - e^{-i\phi})$$

To evaluate the effect of this magnetic dipolar coupling, we will assume that it represents a small contribution to the energy that the individual spinning nuclei would have if the interaction were not present, and we can use first-order perturbation theory to calculate the energy. In this case we need only evaluate diagonal matrix elements of the form (see Sec. 2–2, p. 8),

$$\langle \psi_m | \hat{H}_{12} | \psi_m \rangle$$

It is appropriate to take ψ_m to be a product of the individual spin-wave functions.[1] Using α for the spin function of a nucleus of spin $+\frac{1}{2}$ and β for the spin function for a nucleus of spin $-\frac{1}{2}$, we write

$$\psi_{+1} = \alpha(1)\alpha(2) \qquad \psi_{0_a} = \alpha(1)\beta(2) \qquad \psi_{0_b} = \beta(1)\alpha(2) \qquad \psi_{-1} = \beta(1)\beta(2)$$

The subscripts correspond to the total z-component of angular momentum. Actually, since these states differ only in the orientation of the angular-momentum vector, they are degenerate in the first approximation (i.e., neglecting $\hat{H}_{12}$) and any linear combination of them is also an appropriate zeroth-order solution.[2] It is convenient to choose the set,

$$\psi_{s_{+1}} = \alpha(1)\alpha(2) \tag{4–15a}$$

$$\psi_{s_0} = \alpha(1)\beta(2) + \beta(1)\alpha(2) \tag{4–15b}$$

$$\psi_{s_{-1}} = \beta(1)\beta(2) \tag{4–15c}$$

$$\psi_{a_0} = \alpha(1)\beta(2) - \beta(1)\alpha(2) \tag{4–15d}$$

The subscripts s and a denote symmetric and antisymmetric respectively, the assignment being made on the basis of whether the wave function is unaffected, or changes sign, when the spins are interchanged. The reason we have used this particular choice of functions is that *no transitions between symmetric and antisymmetric states are allowed*, as can be readily

---

[1] This is a perfectly general result for systems which do not interact too strongly, and it can readily be justified as follows: The Hamiltonian for a system composed of two weakly interacting systems can be written as

$$\hat{H} = \hat{H}_1 + \hat{H}_2 + \hat{H}_{12}$$

If we assume that $\hat{H}_{12}$ is small, the Hamiltonian can be approximately written as the sum of the two independent terms, which are assumed individually to have solutions of the form,

$$\hat{H}_1\psi_1 = E_1\psi_1 \qquad \text{and} \qquad \hat{H}_2\psi_2 = E_2\psi_2$$

Assuming a product solution, we write

$$\hat{H}\psi = (\hat{H}_1 + \hat{H}_2)\psi_1\psi_2 = \hat{H}_1\psi_1\psi_2 + \hat{H}_2\psi_1\psi_2 = \psi_2(\hat{H}_1\psi_1) + \psi_1(\hat{H}_2\psi_2)$$
$$= \psi_2 E_1\psi_1 + \psi_1 E_2\psi_2 = (E_1 + E_2)\psi_1\psi_2 = E\psi$$

(Note that ψ_2 is a constant with respect to operations involving the coordinates of system 1, and vice versa.) This justifies our writing, as a first approximation, the solutions

$$\psi = \psi_1\psi_2 \qquad E = E_1 + E_2$$

[2] The justification for this is almost trivial. We write

$$\psi = c_1\psi_1 + c_2\psi_2 + \cdots$$

where

$$\hat{H}\psi_1 = E_1\psi_1, \hat{H}\psi_2 = E_1\psi_2, \ldots$$

Then

$$\hat{H}\psi = \hat{H}(c_1\psi_1 + c_2\psi_2 + \cdots) = c_1\hat{H}\psi_1 + c_2\hat{H}\psi_2 + \cdots$$
$$= c_1 E_1\psi_1 + c_2 E_1\psi_2 + \cdots = E_1(c_1\psi_1 + c_2\psi_2 + \cdots) = E_1\psi$$

seen by evaluation of the matrix elements of $\hat{I}_{\omega}$ (see Eq. 3–44). Since transitions to and from ψ_{a_0} are not allowed, we need only evaluate the diagonal matrix elements of $\hat{H}_{12}$ by using $\psi_{s_{+1}}$, ψ_{s_0}, and $\psi_{s_{-1}}$ to investigate the effect of this first-order perturbation on the magnetic resonance spectrum.

Using previously given rules for the evaluation of matrix elements, it is readily found that only terms involving A and B in Eqs. 4–14 contribute

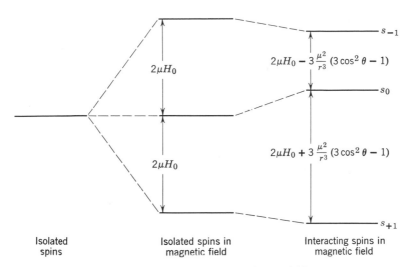

Fig. 4–8   Energy-level diagram for two interacting nuclei in a magnetic field.

to this degree of approximation. Specifically, we find that

$$\langle \psi_{s_{+1}} | \, \hat{H}_{12} \, | \psi_{s_{+1}} \rangle = \frac{-\gamma_N{}^2 \hbar^2}{4r^3}(3\cos^2\theta - 1) = -\frac{\mu^2}{r^3}(3\cos^2\theta - 1)$$

$$\langle \psi_{s_0} | \, \hat{H}_{12} \, | \psi_{s_0} \rangle = \frac{2\gamma_N{}^2 \hbar^2}{4r^3}(3\cos^2\theta - 1) = \frac{2\mu^2}{r^3}(3\cos^2\theta - 1)$$

$$\langle \psi_{s_{-1}} | \, \hat{H}_{12} \, | \psi_{s_{-1}} \rangle = \frac{-\gamma_N{}^2 \hbar^2}{4r^3}(3\cos^2\theta - 1) = -\frac{\mu^2}{r^3}(3\cos^2\theta - 1)$$

Combining this with the external-field-interaction terms, we can construct Fig. 4–8, from which it is obvious that magnetic resonance absorption occurs in the coupled systems for energies such that

$$h\nu = 2\mu H_0 \pm 3\frac{\mu^2}{r^3}(3\cos^2\theta - 1) \qquad (4\text{--}16)$$

Since resonance occurs at $h\nu = 2\mu H_0$ in the absence of dipolar coupling, the effect of this interaction is to cause a splitting into two peaks which occur at the field strengths

$$H = H_0 \pm \frac{3}{2} \frac{\mu}{r^3} (3 \cos^2 \theta - 1) \qquad (4\text{-}17)$$

Studies of the NMR signal of a crystalline sample can thus be used to deduce the separation between a pair of nuclei r as well as the orientation of the radius vector with respect to the field direction θ.

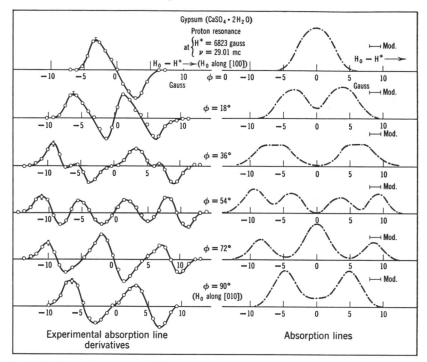

Fig. 4–9   Broad-line proton NMR spectra of gypsum single crystals. [Reproduced by permission from G. E. Pake, *J. Chem. Phys.*, **16**, 327 (1948).]

An analysis such as the foregoing can be applied, for example, to the interaction between the proton pairs in the CH_2Cl groups of 1,2-dichloroethane. A further example is provided by hydrated salt crystals, in which the water molecules are sufficiently separated so that intermolecular interactions produce only small broadening effects. Gypsum samples ($CaSO_4 \cdot 2H_2O$) were studied by Pake, who found that there are two sets of two lines which are clearly discernible at some crystalline orientations (see Fig. 4–9). These two sets arise from two types of water molecules in the unit cell, which are in general oriented differently with respect to the magnetic field.

Frequently it is impossible, or at least impractical, to study single-crystal samples and we must infer structural information from poly-crystalline, or powder, samples. We assume in this case that the sample is finely enough divided so that a random distribution of crystallites at all possible orientations in the magnetic field is achieved. In this case,

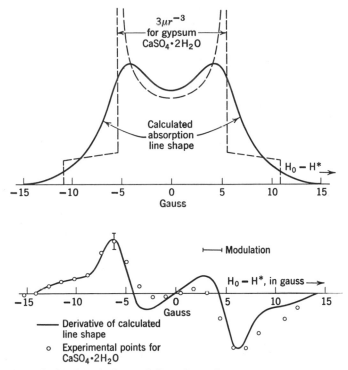

Fig. 4–10   Calculated and observed line shape for proton resonance spectrum of powdered gypsum. [Reproduced by permission from G. E. Pake, *J. Chem. Phys.*, **16**, 327 (1948).]

Eq. 4–17 must be averaged over all values of θ, so that this parameter can no longer be determined. This averaging leads to absorption over a range of field strength, the form of which is shown as the dotted curve in Fig. 4–10. The calculated absorption line includes broadening effects due to unresolved intermolecular coupling, as shown by the solid curve. Although there is a considerable loss of structure in the broadened curve, the peak separation which can be used to determine r is still clearly discernible. Since it is r^3 which enters Eq. 4–17, the determination of r itself remains quite precise even in the polycrystalline samples. The lower curve in Fig. 4–10 shows the derivative curve, with the experimental points obtained by Pake for gypsum.

An analysis such as this can be extended to slightly more complicated systems, although the line shapes become so complex in general that the determination of useful information becomes hopeless. In this case an analysis based on *moments*, as proposed by Van Vleck, can be very useful. The nth moment of an absorption line is defined by

$$S_n = \frac{\int_{-\infty}^{+\infty} h^n f(H)\, dh}{\int_{-\infty}^{+\infty} f(H)\, dh} \tag{4-18}$$

where h is the deviation from the center of absorption, $h = H_0 - H$, and $f(H)$ is the absorption line-shape function. The second moment ($n = 2$) is particularly useful, and can be shown to be of the form

$$S_2 = \frac{3\gamma_N^2 \hbar^2}{2N} I(I + 1) \sum_{j > k} (3\cos^2\theta_{jk} - 1) r_{jk}^{-6}$$

$$+ \frac{\hbar^2}{2N} \sum_{j,f} I_f(I_f + 1)\gamma_{N_f}^2 (3\cos^2\theta_{jf} - 1)^2 r_{jf}^{-6} \tag{4-19}$$

for a single crystal containing nuclei of spin I in resonance. N is the number of resonating nuclei per unit cell, and the second sum is over other species of magnetic nuclei besides those at resonance. For powdered samples, the average over θ gives

$$S_2' = \frac{6\gamma_N^2 \hbar^2}{5N} I(I + 1) \sum_{j > k} r_{jk}^{-6} + \frac{4\hbar^2}{15N} \sum_{j,f} I_f(I_f + 1)\gamma_{N_f}^2 r_{jf}^{-6} \tag{4-20}$$

It is obvious that a complete determination of the structure cannot be made on the basis of a single experimental parameter such as S_2 or S_2'. However, the information can be useful to supplement that available by other techniques. The determination of proton separations, which are not available by X-ray analysis, is a particularly noteworthy example.

Naturally, if a reorientation of nuclei can occur, a narrower signal will be observed since the fields due to dipolar coupling become averaged to a certain extent, and the second moment decreases considerably in such cases. Polycrystalline benzene, which has been studied by Andrew and Eades, serves as an example. The second moment as a function of temperature, as determined by these workers, is shown in Fig. 4–11. The transition in the range 90 to 120°K is attributed to the onset of rotation about the sixfold axis perpendicular to the plane of the ring. A detailed analysis shows that such a reorientation should decrease the contribution of intramolecular broadening to the second moment by a factor

$$\tfrac{1}{4}(3\cos^2\gamma_{jk} - 1)^2$$

where γ_{jk} is the angle which the radius vector between nuclei j and k makes with respect to the reorientation axis. In the case of benzene, $\gamma_{jk} = \pi/2$, and a reduction by a factor of 4 is expected for the second moment. The ratio of the experimental second moments above and below the transition temperature owing to intramolecular coupling (the inter-molecular contribution can be assessed by isotopic substitution tech-niques) is found to be 0.252, in good agreement with that expected on the basis of this model.

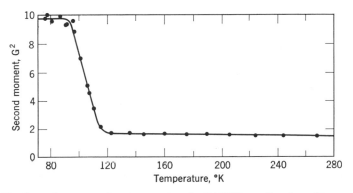

Fig. 4–11   Second moment of proton spectra of solid C_6H_6 as a function of temperature. [Reproduced by permission from E. R. Andrew and R. G. Eades, *Proc. Roy. Soc.*, **218A**, 537 (1953).]

Broad-line NMR spectra frequently show effects which can be ascribed to nuclear-quadrupole interactions. As we have already seen (see Sec. 2–5), nuclear-quadrupole coupling is observable only for nuclei of spin $I \geqslant 1$, where there is a nonvanishing electric-field gradient at the nucleus. The construction of an appropriate Hamiltonian operator from the classical interaction term is a rather involved procedure in this case, so we will merely quote the result:

$$\hat{H}_Q = \frac{eQ}{4I(2I-1)} [V_{zz}(3\hat{I}_z^2 - \hat{I}^2) + (V_{xx} - V_{yy})(\hat{I}_x^2 - \hat{I}_y^2)]$$

Complete asymmetry of the electric field has been assumed here, where V_{zz}, V_{xx}, and V_{yy} are the field gradients along the principal axes,

$$V_{zz} = \frac{\partial^2 V}{\partial z^2} \qquad V_{xx} = \frac{\partial^2 V}{\partial x^2} \qquad V_{yy} = \frac{\partial^2 V}{\partial y^2}$$

It is customary to define a field-gradient parameter q and an asymmetry parameter η by

$$eq = V_{zz} \qquad \eta = \frac{V_{xx} - V_{yy}}{V_{zz}}$$

in which case the Hamiltonian is

$$\hat{H}_Q = \frac{e^2qQ}{4I(2I-1)} [3\hat{I}_z^2 - \hat{I}^2 + \eta(\hat{I}_x^2 - \hat{I}_y^2)] \qquad (4\text{--}21)$$

Deviations from axiality are frequently very small, for which $\eta \approx 0$, and

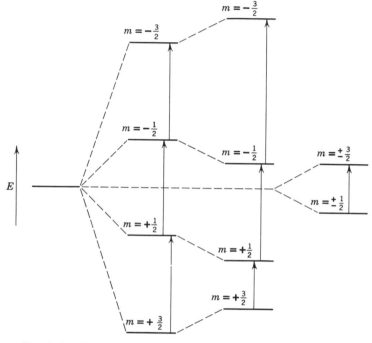

$H_0 = 0,\, Q = 0$ $H_0 \neq 0,\, Q = 0$ $H_0 \neq 0,\, Q \neq 0$ $H_0 = 0,\, Q \neq 0$

Fig. 4–12 Shift of nuclear spin states by nuclear-quadrupole interaction.

the interaction energy correct to first order is

$$E_Q = \frac{e^2qQ}{4I(2I-1)} [3m^2 - I(I+1)] \qquad (4\text{--}22)$$

This leads to a splitting of the NMR signal, as illustrated in Fig. 4–12 for $I = \frac{3}{2}$, from which the quadrupole coupling parameter

$$e^2qQ = eQ \frac{\partial^2 V}{\partial z^2}$$

can be determined. It will be observed that the $m = +\frac{1}{2} \to m = -\frac{1}{2}$ transition is unaffected by the quadrupole interaction to this degree of approximation. It will also be observed that even in the absence of an applied field, there is a splitting of the levels corresponding to $m = \pm\frac{1}{2}$ and $m = \pm\frac{3}{2}$. The induced transitions between these states is termed *pure-quadrupole resonance*, which will be discussed in Chap. 7. We might note in passing that in the absence of an applied field, there is a twofold degeneracy associated with each of the states. This is a general result for half-integral quantum numbers, and illustrates *Kramers theorem* which will be encountered again later (see Chap. 5).

4–3 HIGH-RESOLUTION NMR

In liquid and gas samples, the direct dipolar coupling of nuclear spins, which was discussed in the last section, is ineffective since the rapid tumbling motion of the molecules produces an averaged field at a given nuclear site (indirect interactions can still occur, as we shall see later). It is then possible, in sufficiently homogeneous fields, to distinguish resonance absorption at several field strengths for a given nuclear species within a molecule. The three-line spectrum of ethyl alcohol, with intensities in the ratio $1:2:3$ for the hydroxyl, methylene, and methyl protons, is a well-known example of this. We speak of a *high-resolution spectrum* when such features are distinguishable. Much more structure is observable with present-day high-resolution NMR spectrometers in the case of C_2H_5OH. It is possible, under favorable circumstances, to resolve resonance lines which are separated by a few tenths of a cycle at 60 Mc, which corresponds to a resolution of about one part in 10^8. With such sensitivity, it is possible to deduce very small differences in structural features which are often of considerable interest to the chemist.

Special High-Resolution Techniques

The field homogeneity which can be achieved at the sample position is very frequently the limiting factor in high resolution-NMR spectroscopy. By using appropriately engineered magnetic poles and shim coils, quite uniform fields can be obtained. At best, however, small residual inhomogeneities are still found. A considerable enhancement of the resolution can be achieved by spinning the sample at a sufficient rate. Provided no turbulence is induced, nuclei in the same plane of rotation exhibit a common time-averaged absorption. Rates of the order of 20 to 30 rps are usually satisfactory. This spinning is accomplished by placing on the sample tube a collar which is grooved in such a way that air effusion through jets produces a rotary motion (see Fig. 4–13).

It is seldom necessary to know the absolute field strength of a nuclear resonance signal with great precision. This is fortunate because much more precise measurements can be made if we are only concerned with the *difference* in the field strength of signals. High-resolution NMR spectra are thus calibrated in terms of frequency, or field strength, with respect to some arbitrary zero. Any substance which has a single, well-defined resonance can be used as a standard, such as benzene, chloroform,

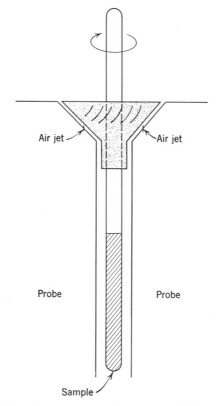

Fig. 4–13 Sample spinner for high-resolution NMR spectroscopy.

cyclohexane, acetone, etc., for proton spectra. We can place a very small quantity of the standard in the sample whose spectrum is of interest, in which case a recorded spectrum will always show the reference peak. Frequently the solvent itself, in a mixture, can be used. We speak of this as an *internal standard*.

An *external standard* is sometimes desired in very precise work. In this case, the standard is separated physically from the sample as, for example, by placing a small, sealed capillary containing the standard in the sample tube. The spectrum will again show both sample and standard resonance peaks, although the latter can be eliminated by carefully shaking the capillary tube to the top of the sample tube, and inverting the tube in such a way that the capillary tube sticks at the top. Although such techniques are more troublesome than those involving the use of internal standards, the possibility of solution effects shifting the reference peak is eliminated.

To obtain a precise calibration with respect to an external reference, a *bulk susceptibility correction* must be made, since the actual magnetic field within the sample will depend on the magnetic polarization near the surface. For a cylindrical tube, it is found that the effective field at a given nuclear site within the sample is

$$H = H_{obs}\left(1 - \frac{2\pi}{3}\chi_v\right) \tag{4-23}$$

where χ_v is the volume magnetic susceptibility previously discussed (Sec. 3–1), and H_{obs} is the observed magnetic-field strength. We often describe the position of a peak in terms of its relative shift in field strength from that of the reference by

$$\delta = \frac{H - H_r}{H_r} \tag{4-24}$$

The shift as described here is a dimensionless quantity, usually expressed in terms of parts per million (ppm). We then find, using Eq. 4–23, that the true shift is

$$\delta = \delta_{obs} + \frac{2\pi}{3}(\chi_{v,r} - \chi_v) \tag{4-25}$$

where $\chi_{v,r}$ and χ_v are the volume susceptibilities of the reference and sample respectively. Values of the volume magnetic susceptibility for numerous substances can be found in the chemical literature. We have listed values for a few of the more commonly used solvents in Table 3–1. Values which cannot be found in the literature can be inferred as discussed in Sec. 3–1, p. 39, or they may be determined by NMR studies with the use of a concentric-tube arrangement.

We have not as yet indicated how the separation of the signal from the standard can be quantitatively determined. The *side-band technique* of Arnold and Packard is generally used for this. This method depends on the fact that, if the magnetic field is modulated with a low-amplitude, a-f signal v', then the resonance signal at v_0 is split into a set of signals,

$$v_0 \pm nv' \qquad n = 0, 1, 2, 3, \ldots$$

The intensity of these additional peaks depends on the amplitude of the a-f modulation. A diagrammatic representation of a typical modulated spectrum is shown in Fig. 4–14. The side bands "rob" intensity from the parent peak, and become vanishingly small for large values of n. If the modulation amplitude is low, only the first side band ($n = 1$) and the parent peak may be observable, whereas if the modulation amplitude is high, the parent peak may be considerably reduced in intensity and the side bands become the most prominent feature of the spectrum.

The side bands are used to calibrate the spectrum by monitoring the frequency of the modulating field. Then, a linear interpolation is used

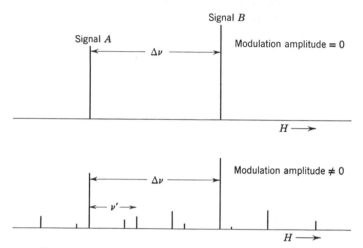

Fig. 4–14. Effect of a side band of frequency v' on a NMR spectrum composed of two resonance peaks.

to determine the frequency of the separation Δv. Naturally, the relative frequency separation defines a dimensionless shift identical to that defined by Eq. 4–24, since

$$\frac{\Delta v}{v_r} = \frac{v - v_r}{v_r} = \frac{\gamma H/2\pi - \gamma H_r/2\pi}{\gamma H_r/2\pi} = \frac{H - H_r}{H_r} = \delta$$

If the sweep is nonlinear, we may vary the modulation frequency to superimpose a side band from the reference standard on the sample peak to determine the separation. For very precise work, the intensity of the sample peak can be plotted *versus* small changes in the modulation frequency as the side band is moved through the sample resonance; the maximum intensity occurs when the side band and sample signal exactly superimpose.

If the magnetic field is inhomogeneous, the nuclei of the sample will pass periodically through varying fields as the sample is spun. The net result is a modulation of the magnetic field which leads to side bands, similar to those generated by the Arnold and Packard technique. These *spinning side bands* have an apparent modulation frequency equal to the sample spinning rate, and can be distinguished from sample absorption peaks by changing the air flow through the spinner. The intensity of a side band, whether intentionally induced or caused by spinning in an inhomogeneous field, decreases as the modulation frequency increases. Thus, spinning side bands can be reduced to insignificant proportions by increasing the spinning rate if the field inhomogeneities are not too large.

Side-band techniques have been used to very good advantage in recent years in the construction of stabilized NMR spectrometers. As we have already mentioned, r-f generators which are constant to about one part in 10^9 are available, but the magnetic field control is not that good and line shifts, noise, and distortions of the NMR signal result. Using a side-band stabilization technique, this difficulty can be overcome by automatic frequency control of the r-f unit.

One of the most popular NMR spectrometers which uses such frequency control is the Varian A-60, a block diagram of which is shown in Fig. 4–15. The side-band oscillator provides a 5 kc signal which is applied through a set of modulation coils in the probe. The spectrometer operates at 60 Mc, so the signal sensed by the control receiver consists of a 60-Mc carrier signal (the proton resonance in an aqueous control sample) plus side bands of 60.005 and 59.995 Mc. Demodulation of the 60-Mc signal is accomplished in the control receiver, and the upper side band is selected as an input to the field modulator unit. Here the audio voltage is amplified, and applied again to the modulating coils, which completes the loop. Now if the field were to decrease slightly, then the effective oscillation frequency would decrease to something less than 60.005 Mc; or if the field increases, the effective r-f frequency increases to something greater than 60.005 Mc. In this way the circuit remains in oscillation and adjusts the side-band frequency to compensate for changes in the field strength. With the r-f frequency thus "locked" to the field strength, reproducible, calibrated spectra can be recorded in quite a routine fashion. Such techniques have done much to make NMR spectroscopy available to chemists in general. One does not have to be an expert in the field to obtain data these days. Spectrometers are also available which lock to the side band of an internal reference, so that separate control samples and analytical samples are not necessary.

In high-resolution spectra, an absorption peak is frequently followed by a set of damped oscillations known as *ringing*. The form of a typical, isolated peak is shown in Fig. 4–16, and it is found that the amount of ringing is directly related to the rate at which one sweeps the magnetic field through resonance. The qualitative explanation of this phenomenon

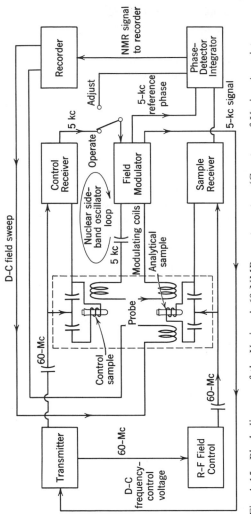

Fig. 4-15 Block diagram of the Varian A-60 NMR spectrometer. (Courtesy of Varian Associates, Palo Alto, Calif.)

is as follows: Under *rapid-passage* conditions, i.e., when Bloch's equations are not followed, the H_1 field turns the magnetization vector away from the strong field direction as before, but at a rate such that **M** is left in a nonequilibrium position after H_1 has increased far past the resonant value. This means that **M** will precess about the H_0 field as it decays exponentially with a time constant T_2. During this time, the magnetization will alternately pass in and out of phase with H_1 because they will be precessing at different rates. If the absorption-mode signal is being observed, the ringing peaks correspond to the passing of the magnetization through the out-of-phase orientation with respect to H_1 as they both rotate about H_0, and a series of damped oscillations is observed. If the field is inhomogeneous, the decay of $\mathbf{M}_{xy}$ is more rapid because of the loss of phase of the individual moments, and the ringing will not be observed. Thus it is the usual practice to use the ringing

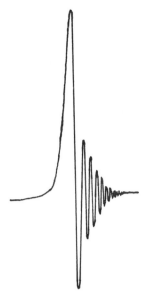

Fig. 4–16   High-resolution NMR absorption peak with ringing.

pattern as a criterion of field homogeneity. Even in the absence of ringing, the peak positions are slightly shifted in a spectrum recorded under rapid-passage conditions. Thus, slow scan rates should always be used for the accurate recording of spectra.

Experimental Parameters

One of the most important molecular parameters determined by NMR is the *chemical shift*. The chemical shift is a measure of the resonance frequency of nuclei in a given chemical environment. In practice, we frequently find that owing to spin interactions with other nuclei, there is a *group* of resonance lines in the region of the chemical-shift value. In such a case the chemical shift may or may not be readily apparent. It can in any case be determined by methods discussed in the next section, and we write, as a quantitative definition, an expression analogous to Eq. 4–24 with H being interpreted as the field strength for resonance in the absence of splitting. Here again, this is equally well defined in terms of frequencies, and, as a matter of fact, chemical shifts are sometimes reported in terms of the frequency difference $\Delta\nu$ (in cycles per second). This is less satisfactory, however, since it does depend on the frequency of the spectrometer. The dimensionless shift $\delta = \Delta\nu/\nu_r$ is thus to be preferred. In practice, v_r is simply replaced by v_0, the operating frequency of the spectrometer, since very small differences are involved.

Since $v = (\gamma/2\pi)H$, it is obvious that the chemical shift expressed as a simple frequency difference is a linear function of the magnetic-field strength, and this suggests that what is involved here is basically of the same nature as the susceptibility effects discussed in Sec. 3–1, p. 35. Thus we think of the field at a given nucleus as being different from the applied field by an amount depending on the local diamagnetic shielding. If this shielding is caused by an induced magnetization, as previously suggested, then it is field-dependent, and we write

$$H_{\text{local}} = H_0(1 - \sigma) \tag{4-26}$$

σ as defined here is called the *shielding constant*, and it serves as an alternative unit in terms of which chemical shifts can be expressed:

$$\delta = \sigma - \sigma_r \tag{4-27}$$

We see that, according to this definition, $\delta > 0$ refers to a shielding in the sample greater than that in the standard, and the resonance is accordingly shifted to higher fields. Similarly, resonances at lower fields than the reference are assigned a negative chemical shift.

Tetramethylsilane (TMS) has been used a great deal as a reference standard for proton resonances in recent years, primarily for two reasons: First, the solvation effects for TMS are very small, so that it can be used as an internal standard by placing a small amount in the liquid to be measured, thereby eliminating the necessity of susceptibility corrections. Secondly, the resonance for most common materials are "down-field" from TMS, so that chemical shifts, relative to TMS, are generally all of the same sign (negative). Another dimensionless scale for chemical shifts, the so-called τ-scale, has been proposed by Tiers and is quite widely used. This scale is defined in such a way that τ values are positive for most δ's, TMS itself having a τ value of 10.

$$\tau = 10 + 10^6\left(\frac{v_{\text{line}} - v_{\text{TMS}}}{v_{\text{spectrometer}}}\right) \tag{4-28}$$

The positions of some common solvents on a dimensionless ppm scale are compared to the positions on a τ-scale in Fig. 4–17.

As already noted, a splitting of spectral lines in addition to that attributable to chemical-shift differences can often be observed under high-resolution conditions. By contrast to the chemical-shift parameter, this further splitting is field independent and is found to be due to a nuclear spin-spin interaction of the form,

$$J_{ij}\mathbf{I}(i) \cdot \mathbf{I}(j) \qquad (4\text{--}29)$$

where $\mathbf{I}(i)$ and $\mathbf{I}(j)$ are spin vectors. J_{ij} is called the *nuclear spin-spin coupling constant*, or simply *coupling constant*, and serves as a measure of the energy of interaction between the nuclei i and j. The coupling constant is usually measured in terms of cycles per second.

J_{ij} is usually quite large for directly bonded nuclei, being frequently of the order of a few hundred cycles per second. It falls off very rapidly

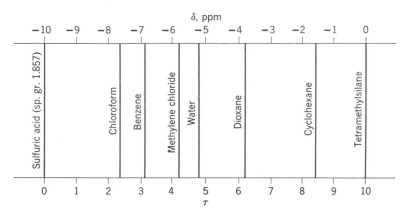

Fig. 4–17 Comparison of dimensionless chemical-shift scale and τ-scale values for several solvents.

with distance for nuclei which are not directly bonded. The mechanism of this coupling has been the subject of considerable investigation, and, although we will discuss it in more detail later, we might note here in passing that it can be qualitatively explained as in indirect interaction through the electrons. A preferential orientation of a given nuclear spin with respect to the electron spin is transmitted through the bonding electrons to other nuclei, which are similarly oriented preferentially with respect to the electron spins. The fact that coupling over several bonds can be observed is a good indication that the valence electrons are correlated to a certain extent to form extended molecular orbitals. Thus, the coupling constant is a parameter that is very sensitive as a measure of certain electronic structural features.

It is convenient to classify spectra of various molecules with respect to the number and type of magnetic nuclei in the molecule. The common convention is to use letters of the alphabet to represent nuclei. Thus, an *AB* spectrum is one which is characterized by two interacting nuclei, which are chemically inequivalent. An example might be the protons in

2-bromo-5-chlorothiophene:

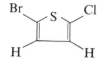

Although this is in fact a four-spin system, the quadrupole relaxation of the halogens is so rapid that coupling to these nuclei does not occur. We designate a spectrum of three interacting nuclei, two of which are equivalent, as an A_2B spectrum, etc. When the chemical-shift difference is very large, there is usually very weak coupling and we use widely separated letters of the alphabet. Thus, the compound $ClCH_2\text{-}CF_2Br$ would be described as an A_2X_2 system. Similarly, an $ABXY$ spectrum has four nuclei, all inequivalent. A and B interact strongly, as do X and Y, but the interactions $A\text{-}X$, $A\text{-}Y$, $B\text{-}X$, and $B\text{-}Y$ are weak. AMX would be used to represent three weakly interacting nuclei, all of which are inequivalent.

In addition to the chemical inequivalence referred to in the foregoing, spectra at times display *magnetic inequivalence*. For example, there are two sets of two chemically equivalent protons in ethylene monothiocarbonate, but there are two *different* couplings between the inequivalent

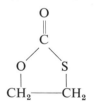

sets. We say that the protons are *magnetically* inequivalent in this case, and sometimes represent the spectrum as $AA'BB'$. Other examples of magnetic inequivalence are provided by the *cis*- and *trans*-2-butenes, which are $A_3A_3'BB'$ spectra. The utility of this classification with respect to magnetic inequivalence arises from the fact that spectra are independent of couplings between magnetically equivalent nuclei, but such couplings can be determined by an analysis of the spectrum if the nuclei are magnetically inequivalent, although they may be chemically equivalent.

Spectrum Analysis

In some cases, we can analyze spectra on the basis of a simple splitting pattern, without any detailed calculation. If the chemical-shift difference is large with respect to the coupling energy, the first-order corrections of the latter to the energy levels will suffice. These corrections are given by (see Eqs. 2–16 and 4–29),

$$\langle\psi_0|\,J_{ij}\hat{\mathbf{I}}(i)\cdot\hat{\mathbf{I}}(j)\,|\psi_0\rangle = J_{ij}\langle\psi_0|\,\hat{I}_z(i)\hat{I}_z(j)\,|\psi_0\rangle$$
$$+\tfrac{1}{2}\langle\psi_0|\,\hat{I}_+(i)\hat{I}_-(j)+\hat{I}_-(i)\hat{I}_+(j)\,|\psi_0\rangle$$
$$= J_{ij}\hbar^2 m_i m_j$$

Thus, for a *first-order analysis*, we need only consider the projection of each nuclear spin along the direction of the applied field.

Let us illustrate the principles involved with the ethyl alcohol spectrum, to which reference has been previously made. We noted that three sets of peaks (ratio 1:2:3) are to be expected on the basis of chemical-shift differences. Rapid rotation about the chemical bonds assures us that the methyl protons are all equivalent (magnetically as well as chemically), as are the methylene protons. Thus, no further splittings result from chemical inequivalence. (This may not be true at temperatures sufficiently low so that rotation ceases.) The methyl protons do interact through spin coupling with the methylene protons, however. Each of the protons of the methylene set can assume two spin states which influence the energy of the methyl protons. Thus, by interaction with the two equivalent methylene protons, the methyl resonance is split into a triplet, with intensity ratios 1:2:1. The spacing between either adjacent pair of peaks

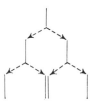

is numerically equal to the magnitude of the coupling constant. In a similar way, we predict a quartet for the methylene protons because of three equivalent splittings by the methyl protons. The intensities within this multiplet are in the ratio 1:3:3:1. In slightly acidified samples,

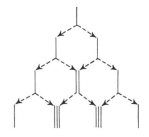

coupling to hydroxyl protons does not occur because of the rapid exchange of the proton, and the spectrum shown in Fig. 4–18 is observed. In highly purified samples, the coupling to the hydroxyl proton further complicates the spectrum.

Splittings between any number of chemically equivalent nuclei can be treated in the same way. It is found for nuclei of spin $I = \frac{1}{2}$ that the intensities are in the ratio of the binomial coefficients for the n-equivalent nuclei, with $n + 1$ lines. In general, there are $2nI + 1$ lines if n-equivalent nuclei of spin I split a resonance line, with the intensities determined by an appropriate multinomial expansion.

An alternative way of looking at this first-order-splitting scheme is as follows: If the nuclei within a given group are all equivalent, then it is only their total resultant spin that is of importance in determining the splitting. For example, for three equivalent nuclei of spin $I = \frac{1}{2}$, the following applies:

(1)	(2)	(3)	$F_z = \sum_i m(i)$
α	α	α	$\frac{3}{2}$
α	α	β	
α	β	α	$\frac{1}{2}$
β	α	α	
α	β	β	
β	α	β	$-\frac{1}{2}$
β	β	α	
β	β	β	$-\frac{3}{2}$

Thus, the group of four lines centered about the chemical-shift position shows equal splittings by a unit amount (in units of J_{ij}), with statistical weights $1:3:3:1$.

Frequently, the coupling energy is of the same order of magnitude as the chemical-shift difference, in which case the first-order analysis is insufficient to account for the observed pattern. We can use perturbation theory and extend the calculation to higher orders. However, unless $|\nu_i - \nu_j| \gg J_{ij}$, the convergence will be slow and the calculation will be quite complex. In this case, a complete solution for the energy levels of the spin system is carried out with a digital computer. The first step to a complete solution is the construction of an appropriate *spin Hamiltonian*. The common convention is to choose the *negative z*-direction along the H_0 field, in which case the energy is $\gamma \hbar H I_z$. This is expressed in ergs, if H is in gauss. Dividing by h converts to cycles per second which is a more convenient unit for our purposes. Thus for a set of nuclei with

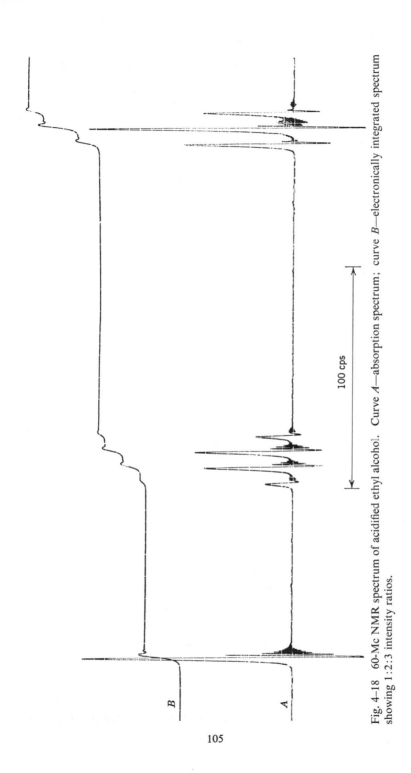

Fig. 4-18 60-Mc NMR spectrum of acidified ethyl alcohol. Curve A—absorption spectrum; curve B—electronically integrated spectrum showing 1:2:3 intensity ratios.

100 cps

magnetogyric ratios γ_i, acted on by fields H_i $[=H_0(1 - \sigma_i)]$, the Hamiltonian is

$$\sum_i \frac{\gamma_i H_i}{2\pi} \hat{I}_z(i) = \sum_i \nu_i \hat{I}_z(i)$$

Combining this with the spin coupling term (Eq. 4–29) gives

$$\hat{H} = \sum_i \nu_i \hat{I}_z(i) + \tfrac{1}{2} \sum_i \sum_{j \neq i} J_{ij} \hat{\mathbf{I}}(i) \cdot \hat{\mathbf{I}}(j) \qquad (4\text{–}30)$$

which is the complete spin Hamiltonian for this case.

We are free to choose a wave function for a variational calculation in any number of ways. A convenient choice is the set of basic product functions for the individual spin states; i.e., the total wave function is of the form

$$\Psi = \sum_i c_i \psi_i \qquad (4\text{–}31)$$

and ψ_i is a product of spin functions, which in the case of nuclei of spin $I = \tfrac{1}{2}$, would be of the form,

$$\psi_i = \alpha(1)\beta(2)\alpha(3) \cdots \beta(p) \equiv \alpha\beta\alpha \cdots \beta$$

for p nuclei. This is but one assignment of spins; in all, there are 2^p terms in the sum (Eq. 4–31) since each nucleus can assume either an α or a β spin.

With this choice of functions, the first-order spectrum is simply obtained from the 2^p diagonal terms of the secular determinant $|H_{ij} - \bar{E}\delta_{ij}| = 0$, derived from Eq. 4–30 (see Sec. 2–2, p, 7). The necessary matrix elements can be readily evaluated by using the information contained in Sec. 2–4. The following rules result:

1. *Diagonal elements* are obtained as a sum of $\pm\nu_i$, the plus or minus sign depending on whether the spin function is α or β; plus the sum of $\pm\tfrac{1}{4}J_{ij}$, the plus or minus sign depending on whether the spins of i and j are parallel or antiparallel. Examples:

$$\langle \alpha\alpha\beta\alpha \,|\hat{H}|\, \alpha\alpha\beta\alpha \rangle = \tfrac{1}{2}(\nu_1 + \nu_2 - \nu_3 + \nu_4)$$
$$+ \tfrac{1}{4}(J_{12} - J_{13} + J_{14} - J_{23} + J_{24} - J_{34})$$
$$\langle \beta\beta\alpha\alpha \,|\hat{H}|\, \beta\beta\alpha\alpha \rangle = \tfrac{1}{2}(-\nu_1 - \nu_2 + \nu_3 + \nu_4)$$
$$+ \tfrac{1}{4}(J_{12} - J_{13} - J_{14} - J_{23} - J_{24} + J_{34})$$

2. *Off-diagonal elements* are zero if the two states differ by more than a single interchange of spins, otherwise it is $+\tfrac{1}{2}J_{ij}$ for the interchanged

pair. Examples:

$$\langle \alpha\beta\alpha| \hat{H} |\alpha\alpha\alpha\beta\rangle = \tfrac{1}{2}J_{34}$$

$$\langle \alpha\alpha\alpha\beta| \hat{H} |\beta\alpha\alpha\alpha\rangle = \tfrac{1}{2}J_{14}$$

$$\langle \alpha\alpha\beta\beta| \hat{H} |\beta\beta\alpha\alpha\rangle = 0$$

In constructing secular equations, it is very useful to note that the operator

$$\hat{F}_z = \sum_i \hat{I}_z(i) \qquad (4\text{--}32)$$

commutes with the spin Hamiltonian, and it can be shown that matrix elements of the Hamiltonian are zero for states corresponding to different eigenvalues of any operator which commutes with the Hamiltonian. This means that mixing between states of different F_z does not occur, and the secular equation is thereby factored into a set of much smaller determinants.

This factoring is not sufficient to give a complete solution in explicit form for any but the simplest cases. Nevertheless, numerical methods are available for solving these matrices which lend themselves to a computer analysis, so that the eigenvalues and eigenvectors of the spin Hamiltonian can readily be found for a given set of chemical shifts and coupling constants.

Having solved the secular equation, it is a simple matter to construct a calculated spectrum. The energy of transition from the state m to the state m' is simply

$$\bar{E}_{m'} - \bar{E}_m$$

and the transition probability is proportional to (see Eq. 3–48)

$$|\langle \psi_{m'}| \sum_i \gamma_i \hat{I}_x(i) |\psi_m\rangle|^2$$

Since the operator here is a sum of single-particle operators, and since matrix elements of $\hat{I}_x$ exist only for states differing by ± 1 in their magnetic quantum number, it follows that the selection rule in this case is

$$\Delta F_z = \pm 1 \qquad (4\text{--}33)$$

The procedure used to analyze a spectrum is as follows: The best possible choice is made for a set of initial values of the chemical shifts and coupling constants. The matrices are constructed and diagonalized, and the calculated NMR spectrum is obtained by using the aforementioned methods. A comparison with the experimental spectrum will usually suggest changes in the parameters which will bring about a correspondence of the calculated and observed spectra. On the basis of the new parameters, the cycle is repeated, and this process continues until the correspondence is as nearly complete as the experimental uncertainties will allow.

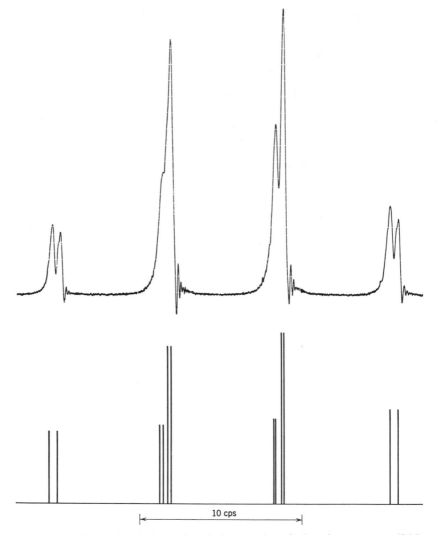

Fig. 4–19   Calculated and observed methylene portion of ethanol spectrum at 60 Mc.

Computer programs have been written by several people which fully automate this procedure so that only experimental data and initial guesses for the parameters have to be supplied, and a computer does the rest. The computation may be somewhat more complicated if there is some arbitrariness in assignments, however. Iterative calculations with all the various possible assignments are often quite time consuming and tedious.

We will not undertake here a discussion of the features of the various spin systems, since these have been presented in many other sources. [A particularly good introductory treatment is given by Roberts (Ref. 7).] We should point out, however, that a complete calculation accounts for higher-order effects which yield additional splittings and shifts that are not present in the first-order treatment. An example of this is shown in Fig. 4–19, where the very high-resolution structural features of the methylene protons in ethyl alcohol are compared with those evaluated by a complete calculation. The higher-order effects are small in this case, but in a more strongly coupled system they may become a very significant part of the analysis. We can, in principle, always obtain a spectrum which is first order to analyze. At sufficiently high fields, the condition $|v_i - v_j| \gg J_{ij}$ will always be fulfilled, since the chemical-shift difference depends on the field strength but the coupling energy does not. It is for this reason that the trend over the past several years has been to construct NMR spectrometers which operate at higher and higher frequencies. We should point out that at high fields some information contained in the higher-order splittings is lost, however. For example, only the magnitude of the coupling constants can be determined at high fields unless decoupling techniques are used. A further elaboration on this point is given in Chap. 6.

Relationship of Experimental Parameters to Molecular Structure

The calculation of shielding constants closely parallels that of diamagnetic susceptibilities given in Sec. 3–1, p. 35. We found that if an atom is placed in a magnetic field, electronic currents are induced in such a way that an opposing field results. The magnitude of this opposing field at the nucleus is

$$- \frac{e^2 \mathbf{H}}{2mc^2 r} \sin^2 \theta$$

Averaging this expression gives

$$- \frac{e^2 \mathbf{H}}{3mc^2} \int \rho(r) \frac{1}{r} \, d\tau = - \frac{4\pi e^2 \mathbf{H}}{3mc^2} \int_0^\infty r \rho(r) \, dr$$

where $\rho(r)$ is the radial distribution function for the electron density. The net field at the nucleus is thus

$$\mathbf{H} - \frac{4\pi e^2 \mathbf{H}}{3mc^2} \int_0^\infty r \rho(r) \, dr = \mathbf{H} \left[1 - \frac{4\pi e^2}{3mc^2} \int_0^\infty r \rho(r) \, dr \right]$$

and it follows from Eq. 4–26 that

$$\sigma = \frac{4\pi e^2}{3mc^2} \int_0^\infty r\rho(r)\, dr \tag{4-34}$$

This is known as *Lamb's formula*. Quite accurate atomic screening constants can be calculated by using atomic wave functions obtained by self-consistent field calculations.

In a molecule, the spherical symmetry is lost, and, just as in the case of susceptibility calculations, the diamagnetic shielding is smaller owing to the hindrance of free rotation. Ramsey has shown that, in this case,

$$\sigma_z = \frac{e^2}{2mc^2} \int \frac{x^2 + y^2}{r^3} \rho\, d\tau + \frac{e^2\hbar^2}{2m^2c^2} \sum_{n\neq 0} \frac{1}{E_n - E_0} \left(\langle\psi_0| \sum_j \frac{\partial}{\partial\phi_j} |\psi_n\rangle \right.$$
$$\times \langle\psi_n| \sum_k \frac{1}{r_k^3} \frac{\partial}{\partial\phi_k} |\psi_0\rangle + \langle\psi_0| \sum_k \frac{1}{r_k^3} \frac{\partial}{\partial\phi_k} |\psi_n\rangle \langle\psi_n| \sum_j \frac{\partial}{\partial\phi_j} |\psi_0\rangle \right)$$

$$\tag{4-35}$$

The mean screening constant is obtained by averaging over all orientations. The first term is entirely analogous to the Lamb formula for atoms, and the second term accounts for the hindrance of free rotation caused by loss of symmetry. It thus vanishes for axially symmetric molecules.

In order to apply Eq. 4–35, we obviously need accurate ground-state and excited-state wave functions. Unfortunately, the latter are not usually available. We can obtain an approximation to Eq. 4–35 which avoids this difficulty by assuming that the excited states are all sufficiently removed from the ground state so that $E_n - E_0$ can be replaced by a *mean excitation energy* ΔE, which is the same for all excited states. With this approximation, the weighting factors in the sum over the excited states is removed, and the sum of the terms in parentheses is simply a product matrix, in which the excited states no longer appear. Thus we obtain

$$\sigma_z = \frac{e^2}{2mc^2} \int \frac{x^2 + y^2}{r^3} \rho\, d\tau + \frac{e^2\hbar^2}{m^2c^2 \Delta E} \langle\psi_0| \sum_{j,k} \frac{1}{r_k^3} \frac{\partial^2}{\partial\phi_j \partial\phi_k} |\psi_0\rangle \tag{4-36}$$

which requires just a knowledge of the ground-state wave function together with the mean excitation energy.

Even with this simplification, the calculation of screening constants in any but the most simple molecules has proved unsuccessful. This is because of the fact that the two terms in Eq. 4–36 are large and of opposite sign, so that, even for quite accurate ground-state wave functions, the errors are magnified to such an extent that no useful calculations are possible.

Thus, we might simply write Eq. 4–36 as

$$\sigma = D - P \tag{4-37}$$

where D is the diamagnetic Lamb-type contribution to the screening and P is the paramagnetic contribution. The parameters D and P are then discussed in a rather empirical, qualitative sense. It is sometimes useful to think of such distinct contributions to the shielding as (1) the diamagnetic contribution of the atom itself, (2) the paramagnetic contribution for the atom itself, and (3) the contribution of all other atoms in the molecule.

An example of how Eq. 4–37 might be used is provided by a study of the cobalt resonance in hexa-coordinated Co^{3+} complexes by Freeman, Murray, and Richards. The chemical shifts are large in this case, being of the order of 2% of the applied field. As discussed in Sec. 2–3, p. 21, the five $3d$ orbitals of cobalt are split by an octahedral field into a set of t_{2g} orbitals and a set of e_g orbitals which differ in energy by an amount Δ (see Fig. 2–6). There are six $3d$ electrons in the Co^{3+} ion, so we obtain a singlet ground state $(t_{2g})^6$ if the crystal-field splitting is large. A transition to a singlet $(t_{2g})^5(e_g)^1$ will be the lowest spin-allowed transition, and this can be characterized by a study of the optical spectrum. Since the operator in the paramagnetic term of Eq. 4–36 does not involve the electron spin, the matrix elements vanish for states of different multiplicity. Hence, we need only consider those excited states corresponding to the promotion of a single electron from the t_{2g} to the e_g orbitals, and we write for the jth member of a set of complexes,

$$\sigma_j = D_j - \frac{B_j}{\Delta j}$$

D_j, the diamagnetic contribution to the screening of the cobalt nucleus, is primarily determined by the inner shells and it is quite insensitive to changes in the ligands. Furthermore, B_j will not be greatly affected by changes in coordination since the matrix elements which are most heavily weighted in P are those involving wave functions close to the cobalt nucleus. Thus, as a first approximation,

$$\sigma_j = D - \frac{B}{\Delta_j}$$

Using this in

$$h\nu_j = \frac{\mu H_j}{I} = \frac{\mu H_0}{I}(1 - \sigma_j)$$

we obtain

$$\nu_j = \frac{\mu H_0}{Ih}\left(1 - D + \frac{B}{\Delta_j}\right)$$

This relationship between NMR frequency and optical transition energy was confirmed by noting a linear relationship between v_j and λ_j, the wave length of optical absorption (note that $\lambda_j \propto 1/\Delta_j$).

The chemical shifts of proton resonances are very small by comparison with other nuclei, being within a range of about 10 ppm (see Table 4–2).

Table 4–2   *Chemical Shifts of Proton Resonances*

Compound	δ, ppm	τ
TMS	0.0	10.0
R_2—NH	$-0.7 - -1.0$	$9.3 - 9.0$
R—CH_3	$-1.0 - -1.6$	$9.0 - 8.4$
R—NH_2	$-1.0 - -2.1$	$9.0 - 7.9$
CH_2 (cyclic)	$-1.4 - -2.0$	$8.6 - 8.0$
=C—CH_3	$-1.7 - -2.0$	$8.3 - 8.0$
Ar—CH_3	$-1.5 - -2.2$	$8.5 - 7.8$
R—SH	$-1.8 - -2.1$	$8.2 - 7.9$
N—CH_3	$-2.3 - -3.1$	$7.7 - 6.9$
≡C—H	$-2.5 - -3.2$	$7.5 - 6.8$
Ar—SH	$-3.0 - -3.3$	$7.0 - 6.7$
Ar_2—NH	$-3.0 - -3.4$	$7.0 - 6.6$
O—CH_3	$-3.5 - -3.9$	$6.5 - 6.1$
Ar—NH_2	$-3.3 - -4.0$	$6.7 - 6.0$
R—OH	$-4.5 - -6.0$	$5.5 - 4.0$
$=C\diagdown{}^R_H$	$-4.7 - -6.9$	$5.3 - 3.1$
Ar—H	$-6.4 - -8.0$	$3.6 - 2.0$
Ar—OH	$-7.3 - -7.9$	$2.7 - 2.1$
RCO_2—NH_2	$-7.9 - -8.3$	$2.1 - 1.7$
R—CHO, Ar—CHO	$-9.5 - -10.2$	$0.5 - -0.2$
R—COOH, Ar—COOH	$-10.8 - -12.4$	$-0.8 - -2.4$
R—SO_3H, Ar—SO_3H	$-11.5 - -12.2$	$-1.5 - -2.2$

The reasons for this small shift are pretty obvious. A hydrogen atom has a very small electron density, so that diamagnetic shielding cannot be expected to be large. Paramagnetic contributions are likewise small, because the excited states are high above the ground state in energy. This means that structural features in other parts of the molecule must be taken into account. An often quoted example of this is the fact that the chemical shifts of ethane, ethylene, and acetylene do not lie in the order to be expected on the basis of proton acidity. As a matter of fact, the acetylenic protons are more shielded than those of either ethane or ethylene. The reason for this has been discussed by Pople and seems to depend on the fact that there are strong paramagnetic circulations perpendicular to the bond axis in acetylene which oppose the diamagnetic circulations along the bond axis. The lines of force for a paramagnetic moment in the bond are of a diamagnetic character at the proton positions, however, and this contribution to the shielding is sufficiently large that acetylene protons are even more shielded than those of ethane (see Fig. 4–20a).

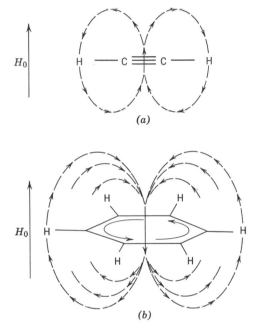

Fig. 4–20   (a) Diamagnetic contribution to proton shielding in alkynes due to the paramagnetic current in the C≡C bond; (b) paramagnetic contribution to proton shielding in aromatic molecules due to ring currents.

A somewhat similar explanation accounts for the fact that aromatic protons are shifted quite far down-field. In this case we think of large, diamagnetic ring currents producing lines of force which augment the applied field at the proton positions, so that the protons come into resonance at a lower value of the applied field (Fig. 4–20b).

Although our account of the chemical-shift parameter is only qualitative in most instances, it is nevertheless a very useful parameter. Tables such as Table 4–2, which are much more extensive, have been compiled by several authors. The chemical shift is strongly influenced by the nature of the grouping in which the nucleus is placed, but it is relatively insensitive to minor changes in molecular structure. Thus, the chemical shift is

Table 4–3   *The Magnitude of Some Representative Hydrogen and Fluorine Coupling Constants for Various Structural Groupings*

Structure	Orientation	$J_{HH'}$, cps	J_{HF}, cps	$J_{FF'}$, cps
	ortho	6–10	6–10	20
	meta	1–3	6–8	2–4
	para	0–1	2	12–15
	geminal	0–3	70–90	27–87
C=C	cis	6–13	1–8	33–58
	trans	12–18	12–40	115–124
C—C	geminal	10–15	40–60	150–400
	vicinal	6–8	0–25	0–25
	geminal	12–14	50	290
	axial-axial	6–12	35–45	—
	axial-equatorial	2–3	0–12	230–300
	equatorial-equatorial	2–3	0–4	—

used nowadays as a characteristic identifying feature in much the same way that IR stretching frequencies have been used in the past.

The chemical-shift and coupling-constant parameters contain structural information which can be regarded as complimentary. The chemical shift, as we have seen, is dependent on the diamagnetic screening at a particular nuclear site, and thus serves as a measure of the electron distribution. The coupling constant, on the other hand, is a measure of the covalent bonding between a given pair of nuclei. In this case, as with the chemical shift, it is found that the coupling constant is primarily determined by immediate structural features and does not vary greatly from compound to compound. This allows us to summarize data such as that shown in Table 4–3, which is diagnostic of the indicated groupings and can be of considerable use for the estimation of initial parameters to be used in the analysis of complex spectra. The reader is again referred to any of a number of NMR reference works for a more complete compilation.

Calculations of coupling constants are usually made following the perturbation approach of Ramsey. It is found that the most important spin-coupling term for molecules which tumble about freely can be represented by a Hamiltonian of the form,

$$\hat{H}_c = \frac{16\pi\beta\hbar}{3}\sum_{k,N} \gamma_N\, \delta(\mathbf{r}_{kN})\hat{\mathbf{S}}_k \cdot \hat{\mathbf{I}}_N \tag{4–38}$$

This is known as a *Fermi contact interaction*, and it derives its name from the fact that the *Dirac delta function* $\delta(\mathbf{r}_{kN})$ assures that the interaction is nonexistent except when the electron k is at the nucleus N. Since only s-type atomic orbitals have a nonzero electron density at the nucleus, it is seen immediately that the contact interaction is very useful for the determination of the extent of s-orbital contribution to various molecular orbitals. This interaction has no classical counterpart; it is one of those characteristic features which have their origin in quantum mechanics, in this case due to relativistic effects.

A comparison of Eq. 4–38 with Eq. 4–29 indicates that nuclear spin-spin coupling is a second-order effect; i.e., we must go to second-order perturbation (see Eq. 2–17a) in which the Hamiltonian is quadratic before a term of the form $\mathbf{I}_N \cdot \mathbf{I}_{N'}$ is obtained. The details of this calculation need not concern us here; the result shows that the second-order contribution of contact coupling to the energy is

$$E_{NN'} = -2\left(\frac{16\pi\beta\hbar}{3}\right)^2 \gamma_N\gamma_{N'} \sum_{n\neq 0}\sum_{k,j}\frac{1}{E_n - E_0}$$
$$\times \langle\psi_0|\,\delta(\mathbf{r}_{kN})\hat{\mathbf{S}}_k \cdot \hat{\mathbf{I}}_N\,|\psi_n\rangle\langle\psi_n|\,\delta(\mathbf{r}_{jN'})\hat{\mathbf{S}}_j \cdot \hat{\mathbf{I}}_{N'}\,|\psi_0\rangle$$

where the sums j and k are over the electrons and n is over the excited states. If we again use the average energy approximation, we can extract the coefficient of $\mathbf{I}_N \cdot \mathbf{I}_{N'}$ and thereby calculate $J_{NN'}$. We obtain

$$J_{NN'} = -\frac{2}{3h}\left(\frac{16\pi\beta\hbar}{3}\right)^2 \gamma_N\gamma_{N'}\frac{1}{\Delta E}\,\langle\psi_0|\sum_{k,j}\delta(\mathbf{r}_{kN})\,\delta(\mathbf{r}_{jN'})\hat{\mathbf{S}}_k \cdot \hat{\mathbf{S}}_j\,|\psi_0\rangle \quad (4\text{–}39)$$

From this we can see explicitly that the coupling is through the electron spins. It can be shown, as a matter of fact, that $J_{NN'}$ is proportional to the excess of electrons of β spin over electrons of α spin at nucleus N', given that there is an electron of α spin at nucleus N. This is, of course, precisely what we mean by a covalent bond.

This interpretation suggests that valence-bond theory might be applicable here, because of the specific manner in which the concept of electron-pair bonding is incorporated. Karplus and Anderson have worked out this valence-bond formulation, which leads to

$$J_{NN'} = \frac{32\beta^2 h}{27\Delta E}\gamma_N\gamma_{N'}\varphi_N(0)\varphi_{N'}(0)\sum_{i,j}c_i c_j\frac{1}{2^{n/2-x_{ij}}}(1 + 2P_{NN'}) \quad (4\text{–}40)$$

where c_i and c_j are the coefficients of the bond functions, $\varphi_N(0)$ and $\varphi_{N'}(0)$ are the electron densities at the N and N' nuclei respectively, and the other terms have been defined in Sec. 2–3, p. 12. Coupling interactions between directly bonded nuclei are not greatly affected by the sum in Eq. 4–40, because the bond order is essentially unity and is only slightly changed by small structural changes. Variations in coupling between directly bonded atoms are thus apt to be reflected through changes in the electron density at the nuclei as well as through changes in the average excitation energy.

On the other hand, the mere fact that coupling occurs between nuclei which are not directly bonded indicates that bonding schemes other than that which pairs strongly overlapping orbitals must be considered. We call this a deviation from *perfect pairing*. Such deviations imply that the approximation of completely localized electron-pair bonds is not valid. Electrons have their spins correlated to a certain small extent from bond to bond, and this delocalized electron bonding gives rise to nuclear spin-spin coupling sometimes over as many as five or six bonds. This electron delocalization can also be interpreted in terms of molecular-orbital theory, but the calculations are somewhat complicated by the uncertainty in the extent to which configuration interaction must be included. Very recent calculations by Pople and Santry have shown considerable promise, however.

One particularly useful application of these theoretical calculations has been in the interpretation of the dependence of coupling constants on small changes in structural features, particularly those related to molecular conformation. One observation immediately apparent by inspection of Table 4-3 is that the size of the coupling constant is not directly related to the distance between the nuclei involved, as might have been supposed. An example is the comparison of *geminal* with *cis* and *trans* couplings in ethylenic compounds, where the *trans* coupling is by far the largest of the three. A similar situation is encountered in saturated hydrocarbons, where it is found that the vicinal coupling is strongly dependent on the dihedral angle. It is found that the coupling passes smoothly from about 8 to 10 cps to zero, and then back up to about 12 to 15 cps as the dihedral angle is varied from 0° (*eclipsed*) to 180° (*trans*) (see Fig. 4–21*a*). (The 6- to 8-cps coupling quoted in Table 4–3 is actually a rotational average.)

We would conclude that the extent of delocalization of electrons depends very strongly on the orientation of the atoms in this case. Using valence-bond methods referred to in the foregoing, Karplus has made calculations based on a simplified model of the form,

in which the dihedral angle was varied from 0° to 180°. It was found that the calculated coupling shows approximately the angular dependence previously noted if only the carbon-carbon exchange interactions are included. This angular-dependent vicinal coupling has similarly been calculated by Conroy using molecular-orbital theory.

A further example of angular-dependent couplings occurs in substituted methanes. The proton-proton coupling is found to depend on the HCH angle, which is influenced by the nature of the carbon atom hybridization, and this, in turn, is determined by the substituents to which the group is

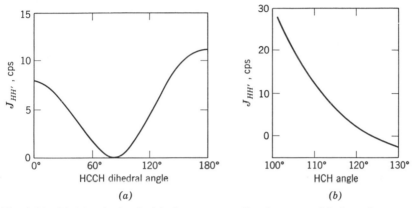

(a)   (b)

Fig. 4–21   (a) Magnitude of vicinal proton coupling in saturated hydrocarbons as a function of the dihedral angle; (b) magnitude of geminal proton coupling as a function of the HCH angle.

bonded (see Fig. 4–21b). Calculations by Gutowsky, Karplus, and Grant using a model of the form

correctly account for the decrease in the magnitude of $J_{HH'}$ as the HCH angle increases. The occurrence of nearby π electrons can have a considerable effect on this correlation, but their effect on the magnitude of the coupling has similarly been accounted for on the basis of a simple model by Barfield and Grant.

We should point out that these calculations are only semiquantitative because of the approximate nature of the molecular wave functions from which they are derived. They can be very useful for qualitative correlations, but it can be dangerous to rely too heavily upon them. In particular, it has recently been shown that the geminal and vicinal couplings in saturated hydrocarbons are of opposite relative sign, with the geminal coupling presumably the negative one (see Sec. 6–1). Although the aforementioned calculations show the correct correlation of the *magnitude* of coupling with molecular conformation, they do predict that both geminal and vicinal couplings are positive. It is likely that this discrepancy is not indicative of any fundamental error in the method, but it is evidence of the extreme caution with which we must view results that are obtained by crude quantum-mechanical calculations.

It would not be possible to include here a complete enumeration of the many applications of the NMR technique in chemistry, but we might mention a few. One of the more notable successes has been in the field of structural analysis, because as we have seen, the NMR parameters are very sensitive to changes of molecular geometry. The structure of molecules which differ only in the relative placement of the constituent atoms is in many cases very difficult to determine by purely chemical means, so that we must frequently rely on physical methods such as X-ray diffraction, optical rotatory dispersion, IR, NMR, and EPR spectroscopy. Both the chemical shift, which depends directly on the electron distribution about a given nucleus, and the coupling constant, which reflects the nature of the bonding between a pair of nuclei, are useful in this regard. Routine organic analysis has been greatly aided by such techniques, with the identification of the configuration of many natural products, such as sugars and steroids, as particularly noteworthy examples.

A more subtle structural problem is involved in conformational analysis. Here the bonding is identical, but the relative orientations of various parts of the molecule are altered by rotations about single bonds. The identification of stable conformers has been greatly facilitated by NMR, principally because of the aforementioned angular dependence of vicinal couplings. Both the *staggered-eclipsed* conformations of straight-chain aliphatic compounds, and the *chair-boat* conformations of ring compounds have been studied in this way.

NMR techniques have been used in the study of some very fast rate processes. If exchange between inequivalent sites takes place, the magnetic resonance absorption may be greatly altered. Often there is a collapse of spin multiplets, and in many other cases a simple coalescing of two resonance peaks, as discussed in Sec. 3–5. The line shape can be used to infer values of the exchange rates, and temperature-dependent studies can also be used to determine the energy of activation of the exchange process. The very elusive protons involved in exchange in alcohols and acids, hydrogen bonding, and keto-enol tautomerism are amenable to study in this way. Rates of restricted rotation about single bonds have also been studied by high-resolution techniques. This is only possible if there are rather large barriers (such as in the amides), however, since it has only been possible to construct probes which operate down to about $-100°C$ thus far.

Although most chemical applications involve high-resolution techniques, broad-line NMR has proved its utility in many instances. In addition to structural and conformational studies of the type mentioned in Sec. 6-2, the application of NMR to such problems as solid-state diffusion and surface adsorption can provide valuable information and should not be overlooked.

SUPPLEMENTARY READING

1. J. A. Pople, W. G. Schneider, and H. J. Bernstein, *High-Resolution Nuclear Magnetic Resonance*, McGraw-Hill Book Company, New York, 1959.
2. E. R. Andrew, *Nuclear Magnetic Resonance*, Cambridge University Press, New York, 1958.
3. R. E. Richards, "Nuclear Magnetic Resonance," in *Advances in Spectroscopy*, H. W. Thompson (Ed.), Interscience Publishers, New York, Vol. II, 1961.
4. J. D. Roberts, *Nuclear Magnetic Resonance. Applications to Problems in Organic Chemistry*, McGraw-Hill Book Company, New York, 1959.
5. L. M. Jackman, *Applications of Nuclear Magnetic Resonance Spectroscopy in Organic Chemistry*, Pergamon Press, New York, 1959.
6. Varian Associates Staff, *NMR and EPR Spectroscopy*, Pergamon Press, New York, 1960.
7. J. D. Roberts, *An Introduction to the Analysis of Spin-Spin Splitting in High-Resolution Nuclear Magnetic Resonance Spectra*, W. A. Benjamin, New York, 1961.

5

Electron Paramagnetic Resonance

The formal theory developed in Chap. 3 is equally applicable to electron paramagnetic resonance (EPR) as well as NMR, although in actual practice the techniques used and the results obtained are quite different. As the name EPR implies, this phenomenon depends on there being a net electronic moment in the species under consideration. Although this severely limits the range of applicability of the EPR method as compared with NMR, there are still numerous problems of chemical interest which fall within the scope of this technique.

A large number of transition metal ions, both with odd and even numbers of electrons, possess net electronic moments which render them paramagnetic and qualify them for this type of study. Odd electron molecules, and organic free radicals with widely varying degrees of stability have been investigated. We might also mention molecules in triplet electronic states, impurities in semiconductors, electrons in unfilled conduction bands, and electrons trapped in radiation-damage sites as further examples of systems which are amenable to EPR study.

5-1 EXPERIMENTAL METHODS

The relationship between frequency and field strength (Eq. 4–1) has been considered in connection with the NMR methods discussed in Chap. 4. The same considerations apply here, the only difference being that the magnetogyric ratio in this case is larger by a factor of the order of 10^3 (see Eq. 2–42). For comparable field strengths, the frequency thus falls in the gigacycle range (1 Gc = 1,000 Mc) rather than the megacycle range. One typically works at field strengths of the order of 3 to 4 kgauss, for which the frequency is about 10 Gc. The corresponding wavelength is about 3 cm, which falls in the so-called X-band of the microwave region. Some work is also done in the K-band, where the frequency is about 18 Gc, as well as in the Q-band, where the frequency is about 35 Gc. The transitions of EPR spectroscopy are ordinarily quite broad compared

with those encountered in NMR work. Thus, field-homogeneity require-
ments are usually less stringent.

Figure 5–1 shows a block diagram of a simple EPR spectrometer. In
principle, the operation is very similar to that described for an NMR

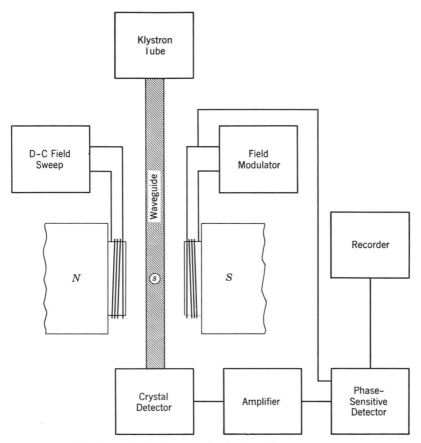

Fig. 5–1   Block diagram of a simple EPR spectrometer.

spectrometer (see Fig. 4–1). The source which provides the oscillating
field is in this case a *klystron tube*, which is an electronic tube wherein
electromagnetic radiation is generated by oscillations set up within a
resonance cavity.

Microwaves cannot be transported effectively by the usual transmission-
line techniques because of the high energy loss by radiation. Thus, tubes
called *waveguides* are used. As the wave travels along the waveguide, it
provides an alternating magnetic field at the fixed position s where the

sample is located. The absorption of energy diminishes the intensity of the microwaves, so that the *crystal detector* receives less microwave power when the resonance condition is fulfilled. This difference is amplified to become the EPR signal. A low-frequency field modulation increases

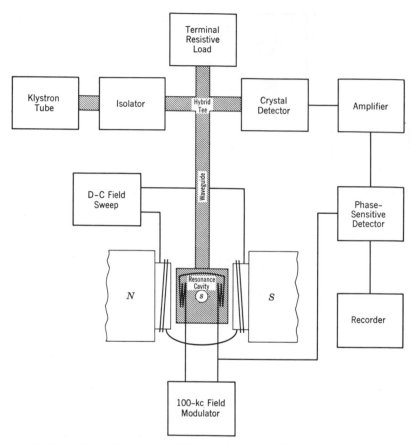

Fig. 5–2   Block diagram of an EPR spectrometer with a microwave bridge.

the sensitivity just as in NMR spectroscopy, with the first derivative of the signal usually being recorded.

Again we are faced with an inherent limitation of the sensitivity which can be achieved with this arrangement and, as before, it stems from the fact that the detector is bathed with the full microwave beam, with the magnetic resonance absorption representing a very small diminution of the total power. In Fig. 5–2 an EPR spectrometer which overcomes this difficulty is illustrated. It employs a microwave bridge which transmits power to the crystal detector only at resonance. In this case, the microwave power passes from the klystron through an *isolator* to the bridge where the power is divided through a *hybrid tee*. The isolator is made of ferrite material which allows transmission to the microwave bridge, but inhibits the reverse transmission. This prevents the klystron from becoming detuned when the bridge is unbalanced at resonance. The sample is placed in a *resonance cavity*, which is a hollow enclosure of such dimensions that an oscillating microwave field can be maintained by proper coupling to the bridge. This coupling is through a small orifice called the *iris*, the size of which is adjusted so that little microwave power leaves the cavity, but sufficient power can enter to replace that which is dissipated through the walls. The sample is placed in the cavity in such a position that it is acted upon effectively by the magnetic field of the microwaves. The absorption of energy from this field results in an imbalance which allows power to be transmitted to the crystal detector. Here, as before, the signal is demodulated and then amplified. We have also indicated in Fig. 5–2 an increase in frequency of the field modulation to 100 kc, which increases the sensitivity.

For some applications, it is useful to increase further the sensitivity by the use of a *superheterodyne*. This employs two klystrons, which operate at a certain, fixed frequency difference. This frequency difference (usually about 60 Mc) is called the *intermediate frequency* (IF), and it carries the EPR signal in much the same way as the side bands discussed in the previous chapter. A much improved signal-to-noise ratio can be achieved by amplification in the 60-Mc range, so a more sensitive detection system is obtained.

Solid, liquid, or gaseous samples can be used in EPR spectroscopy, the first two being more commonly employed. The samples are usually enclosed in quartz tubes, since glass contains a sufficient quantity of paramagnetic impurities to interfere in many cases. In the next section we will discuss the nature of the data obtained from solid and liquid samples.

Some special techniques are needed to observe radical species which have limited stability. Transient radicals have been generated *in situ* in a number of ways, among which are the following:

Optical radiation. Some radicals can be produced by photochemical action. This is possible at times in the visible, but it occurs more commonly in the ultraviolet. Cavities can be constructed which allow this radiation with the sample in position.

Ionizing radiation. Molecular fragments of interest can often be produced by X-rays or γ-rays. It is sometimes advantageous to drill holes in the pole caps of the magnet so that the sample can be irradiated along the field direction. Linear and Van de Graaf accelerators have been used recently to produce electron beams for bombardment of hydrocarbons with the production of free radicals. In this case the cavity can be filled with the sample.

Electrolysis. Sample cells can be constructed which allow the EPR spectra to be recorded of species produced either by electrolytic oxidation or reduction.

Flow systems. Rapid-flow mixing chambers can be used to observe transient radicals which occur as reaction intermediates. Steady-state concentrations of these radicals can be observed in a sample cell which allows the EPR signal to be recorded as the samples mix and pass through the cavity.

With the use of a transfer oscillator and counter, it is possible to monitor the frequency of the microwave field during the recording of spectra. The field strength is frequently determined with a small NMR probe. By observation of the frequency at which nuclear resonance in a standard sample occurs, accurate field calibrations are possible. Spectra can also be calibrated by the superposition of a standard signal on the spectrum of interest. The sample can be "doped" with the standard or it can be placed in an adjoining dual-cavity arrangement, and the two signals can be recorded simultaneously with a dual-channel strip-chart recorder. DPPH (diphenyl picryl hydrazyl) is often used as a standard. It has a resonance absorption which corresponds to a g value of 2.0035 (see Eq. 2–42). The peroxylamine disulfonate ion, $ON(SO_3)_2^=$, is also used frequently. It has three hyperfine lines due to nitrogen hyperfine coupling which have a splitting of 13.0 gauss. The peaks are centered at a g value of 2.0057. A solution of a compound such as vanadium (II) chloride can be used to calibrate the much broader signals encountered in transition metal complexes.

5–2 EPR SPECTRA AND THEIR ANALYSIS

As with NMR spectra, the analysis of EPR spectra can be carried out based on a spin Hamiltonian. We will discuss the analysis in this section from a phenomenological viewpoint, reserving for Sec. 5–3 a consideration of how the parameters relate to molecular structure.

The Spin Hamiltonian

In the moderately strong magnetic fields employed in EPR spectroscopy, the indirect interaction of the electronic moment with the magnetic field (the Zeeman effect) is usually predominant. If the electronic moment were caused by spin alone, with no orbital contribution, we would write for the energy of this interaction (see Sec. 2–4)

$$2.0023\beta_M \mathbf{H} \cdot \mathbf{S}$$

We can conveniently include the effect of orbital contributions by introducing an effective spin $\mathbf{S}'$, with the Zeeman interaction being written

$$g\beta_M \mathbf{H} \cdot \mathbf{S}' \tag{5-1}$$

g is the spectroscopic splitting factor previously defined (Sec. 2–4). Only in a free atom or ion is the orbital moment isotropic, however, so the operator corresponding to Eq. 5–1 must be generalized to read

$$\beta_M \mathbf{H}^\dagger \cdot \mathbf{g} \cdot \hat{\mathbf{S}}' \tag{5-2}$$

where $\mathbf{H}^\dagger$ is a row vector, being the transpose of $\mathbf{H}$, and $\mathbf{g}$ is a second rank tensor which takes account of the fact that the effective spin may be quantized along an effective field which is different than that externally applied. The means by which this alteration of the effective field takes place is spin-orbit coupling, i.e., the interaction of the moments associated with spin and orbital motion.

$\mathbf{g}$ is actually a 3×3 symmetric matrix, which can be represented by

$$\mathbf{g} = \begin{pmatrix} g_{11} & g_{12} & g_{13} \\ g_{12} & g_{22} & g_{23} \\ g_{13} & g_{23} & g_{33} \end{pmatrix} \tag{5-3}$$

By a rotation of coordinates, this can always be transformed to a coordinate system in which the g tensor is diagonal, i.e.,

$$\mathbf{g} = \begin{pmatrix} g_{xx} & 0 & 0 \\ 0 & g_{yy} & 0 \\ 0 & 0 & g_{zz} \end{pmatrix} \tag{5-4}$$

g_{xx}, g_{yy}, and g_{zz} are known as the principal values of the g tensor. If $g_{xx} \neq g_{yy} \neq g_{zz}$, we speak of complete anisotropy; if $g_{xx} = g_{yy} \neq g_{zz}$, the g tensor is axially symmetric; and if $g_{xx} = g_{yy} = g_{zz}$, the g tensor is isotropic. In the axially symmetric case, we always choose the symmetry axis to be the z-axis, and define components parallel and perpendicular to this axis by $g_{zz} = g_{\parallel}$, $g_{xx} = g_{yy} = g_{\perp}$.

Spectra frequently show hyperfine interactions with magnetic nuclei, if such are present in the molecule. This interaction can take place by two quite distinct mechanisms. The first is the ordinary classical dipolar interaction of the type encountered in Sec. 4–2. In this case, it can be written as

$$-gg_N\beta_M\beta_N\left[\frac{\mathbf{I}\cdot\mathbf{S}'}{r^3} - 3\frac{(\mathbf{I}\cdot\mathbf{r})(\mathbf{S}'\cdot\mathbf{r})}{r^5}\right] \tag{5-5}$$

The second has also been encountered before (Sec. 4–3, p. 114); it is the Fermi contact interaction

$$\frac{8\pi}{3}\,gg_N\beta_M\beta_N\,\delta(\mathbf{r})\mathbf{I}\cdot\mathbf{S}' \tag{5-6}$$

which describes an isotropic interaction with s electrons. We generally have insufficient knowledge of the molecular wave functions to calculate the magnitude of these interactions from first principles. Thus, we write the expectation value of these operators in the spin Hamiltonian in terms of electron and nuclear spin operators, together with certain molecular parameters:

$$\langle\psi_0|\,\hat{H}_{Is'}\,|\psi_0\rangle = \hat{\mathbf{S}}'\cdot\mathbf{B}\cdot\hat{\mathbf{I}} + A\hat{\mathbf{S}}'\cdot\hat{\mathbf{I}} \tag{5-7}$$

where

$$A = gg_N\beta_M\beta_N\,\frac{8\pi}{3}\,\psi_0{}^2|_{r=0} \tag{5-8}$$

and

$$\mathbf{B} = gg_N\beta_M\beta_N\left\langle\psi_0\left|\,\frac{3\mathbf{rr}}{r^5} - \tau\,\frac{1}{r^3}\,\right|\psi_0\right\rangle \tag{5-9}$$

$\psi_0{}^2|_{r=0}$ is the electron density at the nucleus and τ is the unit dyadic, which is the sum of the components of a 3×3 unit matrix. The scalar A obviously comes from the contact interaction, and $\mathbf{B}$ is a traceless, second-rank tensor which arises from the dipolar interaction (Eq. 5–5).

Other terms may need to be included in an analysis. For example, a splitting of the energy levels sometimes occurs which is independent of the magnetic field. This is called the *zero-field-splitting* term, and is written as

$$\hat{\mathbf{S}}'^\dagger\cdot\mathbf{D}\cdot\hat{\mathbf{S}}' \tag{5-10}$$

This may be regarded as an interaction between unpaired electrons, which vanishes for $|\mathbf{S}'| = \frac{1}{2}$. The nuclear-energy states may be shifted by a nuclear quadrupole interaction (see Secs. 2–5 and 4–2) or by direct interaction with the applied field $g_N\beta_N\mathbf{H}\cdot\hat{\mathbf{I}}$. These corrections can be incorporated when necessary, but for many cases, the spin Hamiltonian can be taken simply as

$$\hat{H} = \beta_M\mathbf{H}^\dagger\cdot\mathbf{g}\cdot\hat{\mathbf{S}}' + \sum_k \hat{\mathbf{S}}'^\dagger\cdot\mathbf{A}_k\cdot\hat{\mathbf{I}}_k \tag{5-11}$$

where the sum is over the magnetic nuclei in the molecule. The two hyperfine coupling terms have been combined into a single second-rank tensor defined by

$$A_{ij} = B_{ij} + A\delta_{ij}$$

for each nucleus, where δ_{ij} is the Kronecker delta. We will restrict our subsequent discussion of this section to the spin Hamiltonian defined by Eq. 5–11.

Solid-State Spectra

Let us assume that the same coordinate transformation which diagonalizes the g tensor also diagonalizes the hyperfine tensors. This is not always so, but it does apply in many cases, since the principal axis systems for these tensors must coincide with symmetry axes which are present in the molecule. Then, in the principal-axis coordinate system, the spin Hamiltonian is

$$\hat{H} = \beta_M(g_{xx}H_x\hat{S}'_x + g_{yy}H_y\hat{S}'_y + g_{zz}H_z\hat{S}'_z)$$
$$+ \sum_k (A_{xxk}\hat{S}'_x\hat{I}_{xk} + A_{yyk}\hat{S}'_y\hat{I}_{yk} + A_{zzk}\hat{S}'_z\hat{I}_{zk}) \quad (5\text{–}12)$$

Writing the magnetic field in polar coordinates,

$$\mathbf{H} = H\begin{pmatrix} \sin\theta\cos\phi \\ \sin\theta\sin\phi \\ \cos\theta \end{pmatrix}$$

the Zeeman term becomes

$$g(\theta,\phi)\beta_M H(l_x\hat{S}'_x + l_y\hat{S}'_y + l_z\hat{S}'_z)$$

where

$$l_x = \frac{1}{g(\theta,\phi)}(g_{xx}\sin\theta\cos\phi) \qquad l_y = \frac{1}{g(\theta,\phi)}(g_{yy}\sin\theta\sin\phi)$$

$$l_z = \frac{1}{g(\theta,\phi)}g_{zz}\cos\theta$$

$$g(\theta,\phi) = (g_{xx}^2\sin^2\theta\cos^2\phi + g_{yy}^2\sin^2\theta\sin^2\phi + g_{zz}^2\cos^2\theta)^{\frac{1}{2}} \quad (5\text{–}13)$$

l_x, l_y, and l_z are the direction cosines defining the angle which the *effective* field makes with respect to the principal-axis system. A rotation of coordinates of the electron to the effective field coordinates leaves the Zeeman-term diagonal:

$$g(\theta,\phi)\beta_M H\hat{S}''_z \quad (5\text{–}14)$$

We will regard this as the zeroth-order Hamiltonian for a perturbation calculation, since the nuclear moments are small and generally have little influence on the energy. To this degree of approximation, the energy of a given state, which is characterized by the magnetic quantum number M'', is

$$\langle \psi_0 | g(\theta, \phi)\beta_M H \hat{S}''_z | \psi_0 \rangle = g(\theta, \phi)\beta_M H M'' \qquad (5\text{-}15)$$

As usual, only single quantum transitions are allowed, so the absorption energy is given by

$$h\nu = E_{M''} - E_{M''-1} = g(\theta, \phi)\beta_M H M'' - g(\theta, \phi)\beta_M H(M'' - 1)$$
$$= g(\theta, \phi)\beta_M H \qquad (5\text{-}16)$$

By treating the polar angles and g_{xx}, g_{yy}, and g_{zz} as parameters, the g tensor can be specified, both with respect to magnitude and orientation.[1] This is done by noting the g values for resonance absorption by a single crystal for a known field strength and microwave frequency. In principle, we need measurements at as many orientations of the crystal as there are unknowns; in practice, many more measurements are often needed.

In magnetically concentrated samples, it is only this zeroth-order interaction which is observed. This is because the interaction between neighboring paramagnetic ions allows the electron spins to reorient with sufficient rapidity that nuclear coupling is ineffective. There are other factors to consider in concentrated samples as well. We might have expected very broad signals owing to dipolar interactions between molecules, but, in fact, quite narrow peaks are observed. The reason for this, as shown by Van Vleck, is that there is a compensation for the effect of dipolar broadening by quantum-mechanical exchange interactions. These *exchange-narrowed* signals are generally Lorentzian in form, although the various broadening effects (see Sec. 3–2, p. 50) in more dilute samples frequently, but not always, lead to Gaussian-shaped peaks.

Thus, magnetically dilute samples must be prepared in order to observe the hyperfine coupling. Radicals which are generated by techniques such as those mentioned in Sec. 5–1 will fulfill this requirement in most cases. To achieve magnetic dilution with a chemically stable, paramagnetic species, it may be necessary to introduce it as an impurity in a diamagnetic matrix. Distortions by the foreign matrix may be appreciable unless a very similar substance is used as the magnetic diluent.

The hyperfine terms are handled by a very similar procedure. The direction cosines for the nuclear interaction terms are

$$L_{x_k} = \frac{A_{xx_k} l_x}{K_k(\theta, \phi)} \qquad L_{y_k} = \frac{A_{yy_k} l_y}{K_k(\theta, \phi)} \qquad L_{z_k} = \frac{A_{zz_k} l_z}{K_k(\theta, \phi)}$$

---

[1] The *complete* specification of the orientation of the principal axes would, of course, involve *three* angles, such as the Eulerian angles.

where

$$K_k(\theta, \phi) = \frac{1}{g(\theta, \phi)} (A_{xx_k}^2 g_{xx}^2 \sin^2 \theta \cos^2 \phi$$
$$+ A_{yy_k}^2 g_{yy}^2 \sin^2 \theta \sin^2 \phi + A_{zz_k}^2 g_{zz}^2 \cos^2 \theta)^{\frac{1}{2}} \quad (5\text{--}17)$$

Retaining only first-order perturbation terms, the hyperfine interaction energy is found to be

$$\langle \psi_0 | \sum_k K_k(\theta, \phi) \hat{S}_z'' \hat{I}_z' | \psi_0 \rangle = \sum_k K_k(\theta, \phi) M'' m_k'$$

Here m_k' is the nuclear magnetic quantum number, which takes on values between $+I$ and $-I$ in integral steps. Thus, the transition energies are given by

$$h\nu = g(\theta, \phi)\beta_M H + \sum_k K_k(\theta, \phi) m_k' \quad (5\text{--}18)$$

and the spectrum consists of a group of lines centered about the field position $h\nu/g(\theta, \phi)\beta_M$. Each nucleus contributes $2I + 1$ hyperfine lines. Less than the maximum number will be observed owing to degeneracy if some of the nuclei are equivalent. It is the total number of equivalent nuclei in a set that determines the splitting in this case. In a single crystal, the splitting pattern will move "in and out" as the crystal is rotated if the hyperfine coupling is anisotropic, and the entire hyperfine pattern may itself be changing field as the crystal rotates if the g tensor is also anisotropic. A complication frequently encountered is the occurrence of more than one molecule per unit cell. These molecules will usually be inequivalent, except at a few certain orientations, so the observed spectrum is complicated by overlapping sets of lines. It is sometimes useful to rely on a computer analysis in such cases.

It is not always possible, or practical, to work with samples in the form of single crystals. Quite a lot of EPR data has been recorded with the use of amorphous or powdered samples. In this case, the molecules of the sample are randomly oriented with respect to the magnetic-field direction. The line shape is obtained as an average over all angles. Since the spectrum is usually recorded as the first derivative, the line-shape function can be written as

$$\frac{dF}{dH} = \frac{1}{4\pi} \int_0^\pi \int_0^{2\pi} \frac{dL}{dH} \sin \theta \, d\theta \, d\phi \quad (5\text{--}19)$$

Here, L is the individual-component line-shape function; i.e., it is a Gaussian, Lorentzian, δ line-shape function, etc., centered at the resonance field position given by

$$H = \frac{h\nu}{g(\theta, \phi)\beta_M} - \sum_k \frac{K_k(\theta, \phi)}{g(\theta, \phi)\beta_M} m_k' \quad (5\text{--}20)$$

The integration indicated in Eq. 5–19 cannot be carried out in closed form in most cases, but line shapes can be calculated by a numerical integration with a computer. The form of the curves observed in powders is illustrated in Fig. 5–3 for completely anisotropic and axial cases. Such curves may be observed if there is g anisotropy but no hyperfine splitting; in general, however, the observed spectrum is a superposition of several

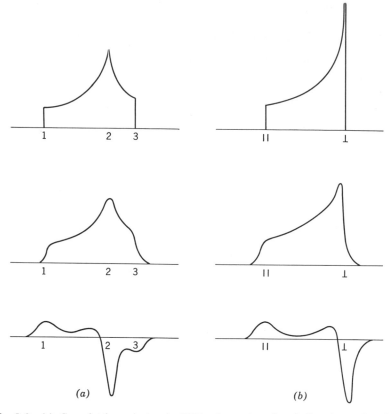

Fig. 5–3   (a) Completely anisotropic EPR absorption for δ line-shape function, broadened absorption, and first derivative of broadened absorption of a powder; (b) axial EPR absorption for δ line-shape function, broadened absorption, and first derivative of broadened absorption of a powder.

such curves (one for each hyperfine component). In such a case, the analysis may be quite difficult, although it can be carried out by an iterative procedure in which calculated curves are matched to the experimental ones. For such powder spectra, we can determine all the principal values of the g tensor and hyperfine tensors, but, of course, no information concerning the orientation of the principal-axis systems is obtained.

Solution Spectra

In solution the molecules are free to tumble about. The spin Hamiltonian as written in Eq. 5–12 was referred to a principal-axis system fixed in the molecule, but now it must be transformed to a space-fixed reference frame. If the laboratory frame is defined with respect to the principal axes by the polar angles $\gamma_1, \gamma_2, \gamma_3$ and the azimuthal angles $\beta_1, \beta_2, \beta_3$, the transformed Hamiltonian can be shown to be of the form,

$$
\begin{aligned}
\hat{H} = \frac{g_{xx} + g_{yy} + g_{zz}}{3} \beta_M H \hat{S}_z' + \sum_i \Bigg\{ & \frac{A_{xxi} + A_{yyi} + A_{zzi}}{3} \hat{S}' \cdot \hat{I}_i \\
+ & [(\Delta g_{xy} \beta_M H + \Delta A_{xy_i} \hat{I}_{z_i})(\cos^2 \gamma_1 - \tfrac{1}{3}) \\
+ & (\Delta g_{zy} \beta_M H + \Delta A_{zy_i} \hat{I}_{z_i})(\cos^2 \gamma_3 - \tfrac{1}{3})] \hat{S}_z' \\
+ & [\tfrac{1}{2}\Delta A_{xy_i} \sin \gamma_1 \cos \gamma_1 (\hat{I}_{+i} e^{-i\beta_1} + \hat{I}_{-i} e^{+i\beta_1}) \\
+ & \tfrac{1}{2} \Delta A_{xy_i} \sin \gamma_3 \cos \gamma_3 (\hat{I}_{+i} e^{-i\beta_3} + \hat{I}_{-i} e^{+i\beta_3})] \hat{S}_z' \\
+ & \tfrac{1}{2}(\Delta g_{xy} \beta_M H + \Delta A_{xy_i} \hat{I}_{z_i}) \sin \gamma_1 \cos \gamma_1 (\hat{S}_+ e^{-i\beta_1} + \hat{S}_- e^{+i\beta_1}) \\
+ & \tfrac{1}{2}(\Delta g_{zy} \beta_M H + \Delta A_{zy_i} \hat{I}_{z_i}) \sin \gamma_1 \cos \gamma_1 (\hat{S}_+ e^{-i\beta_3} + \hat{S}_- e^{+i\beta_3}) \\
+ & \tfrac{1}{4} \Delta A_{xy_i} \sin^2 \gamma_1 (\hat{S}_+ \hat{I}_{+i} e^{-2i\beta_1} + \hat{S}_- \hat{I}_{-i} e^{+2i\beta_1}) \\
+ & \tfrac{1}{4} \Delta A_{zy_i} \sin^2 \gamma_3 (\hat{S}_+ \hat{I}_{+i} e^{-2i\beta_3} + \hat{S}_- \hat{I}_{-i} e^{+2i\beta_3}) \\
- & \tfrac{1}{4}[\Delta A_{xy_i}(\cos^2 \gamma_1 - \tfrac{1}{3}) + \Delta A_{zy_i}(\cos^2 \gamma_3 - \tfrac{1}{3})](\hat{S}_+ \hat{I}_{-i} + \hat{S}_- \hat{I}_{+i}) \Bigg\}
\end{aligned}
$$

$$(5\text{–}21)$$

where

$$
\begin{aligned}
\Delta g_{xy} &= g_{xx} - g_{yy} & \Delta g_{zy} &= g_{zz} - g_{yy} \\
\Delta A_{xy_i} &= A_{xx_i} - A_{yy_i} & \Delta A_{zy_i} &= A_{zz_i} - A_{yy_i}
\end{aligned}
$$

and H as usual defines the z-direction.

The γ's and β's must now be considered to be functions of time. Let us denote the frequency of molecular tumbling by ν_t, and the frequency of nuclear precession by ν_n. Then, if $\nu_n \gg \nu_t$, the molecule can be regarded as fixed in space through many periods of nuclear precession, and what is observed is a typical solid-state spectrum characterized by the eigenvalues of the full Hamiltonian (Eq. 5–21), or the equivalent (Eq. 5–12). In the other limit, i.e., $\nu_n \ll \nu_t$, the molecule passes through all orientations of the external field many times during one period of nuclear precession, so all the angular-dependent terms in Eq. 5–21 ought to be replaced by their average values. It can readily be verified that

$$
\overline{(\cos^2 \gamma_i - \tfrac{1}{3})} \equiv \frac{1}{4\pi} \int_0^{2\pi} \int_0^{\pi} (\cos^2 \gamma_i - \tfrac{1}{3}) \sin \gamma_i \, d\gamma_i \, d\beta_i = 0
$$

and similarly,

$$\overline{\sin \gamma_i \cos \gamma_i e^{\pm i\beta_i}} = \overline{\sin^2 \gamma_i e^{\pm 2i\beta_i}} = 0$$

This leaves only

$$\hat{H} = g_s\beta_M H\hat{S}'_z + \sum_i A_{s_i}\hat{S}' \cdot \hat{I}_i \tag{5-22}$$

as the spin Hamiltonian for solutions, where g_0 and A_{0_i} are just the average values of the g tensors and hyperfine coupling tensors defined by

$$g_s = \tfrac{1}{3}\operatorname{Tr} \mathbf{g} = \frac{g_{xx} + g_{yy} + g_{zz}}{3}$$

$$A_{s_i} = \tfrac{1}{3}\operatorname{Tr} \mathbf{A}_i = \frac{A_{xxi} + A_{yyi} + A_{zzi}}{3} \tag{5-23}$$

The intermediate case ($v_n \approx v_t$) applies to viscous solutions where the averaging caused by tumbling is only partially complete. This intermediate case constitutes a very formidable problem with which we will not concern ourselves.

Solution spectra are thus characterized by a set of resonance lines centered about the field strength given by $hv/g_s\beta_M$. Correct to first order, these lines occur at the positions,

$$\frac{hv}{g_s\beta_M} - \sum_i \frac{A_{si}}{g_s\beta_M} m_i$$

In general, there are

$$\prod_i (2n_iI_i + 1)$$

lines, where n_i is the number of equivalent nuclei, each with spin I_i, and the product is over the sets of equivalent nuclei within the molecule. The intensities are given by an appropriate multinomial expansion.

It is important to note that only the contact coupling contributes to the hyperfine splitting in this case. This is readily observed by noting that

$$A_{si} = \tfrac{1}{3}\operatorname{Tr} \mathbf{A}_i = \tfrac{1}{3}\operatorname{Tr} \mathbf{B}_i + A_i = A_i$$

since, as we have already mentioned, $\mathbf{B}$ is a traceless tensor.

Solution studies are very useful to supplement data obtained from the solid state. Eq. 5–23 gives a relationship between the parameters g_{xx}, g_{yy}, and g_{zz} which can be used to aid in an analysis of the anisotropic components. The isotropic parameters determined from solution spectra are, of course, of interest in their own right. This is particularly true of the hyperfine terms, which in this case are determined solely by the contact-coupling interaction. Since the classical dipolar interaction yields a traceless tensor, these two interactions can be readily distinguished if the full tensors are known, however, so the complete solid-state data should be regarded as preferable. The price we pay for this extra information is a great deal of additional complexity in the experimental work and/or the interpretation of solid-state spectra.

5–3 RELATIONSHIP OF EXPERIMENTAL PARAMETERS TO MOLECULAR STRUCTURE

We divide the following discussion into two sections—inorganic complexes and organic radicals. Actually there is no fundamental difference in the processes involved, but it is profitable in practice to follow the lead of the successful valence-theory approaches in the interpretation of EPR data, and we have seen that these proceed along somewhat different lines (Sec. 2–3). Excellent discussions of these topics can be found in Refs. 8 and 9.

Inorganic Complexes

As we have already indicated, the magnetic properties of the transition metal ions are strongly influenced by the crystal fields produced by the ligands. The details of the splitting of the electronic-energy levels depend on the symmetry of the crystal field as well as on the relative magnitude of the spin-orbit coupling, which we will represent as $\lambda \mathbf{L} \cdot \mathbf{S}$. Let us denote the crystal-field interaction energy by V. There are three categories of complexes to consider:

1. $V < \lambda \mathbf{L} \cdot \mathbf{S}$. In this *weak-field case* we obtain, in effect, a set of atomic-energy levels with small crystal-field perturbations. Such a situation is encountered in the rare earths, for example, where the unfilled f shells are relatively deep within the electronic structure of the atom and are thus quite well shielded from the crystal field. This is in essence a problem in atomic spectroscopy with a weak electric field applied (the Stark effect).
2. $\lambda \mathbf{L} \cdot \mathbf{S} < V < e^2/r_{ij}$. This is the so-called *intermediate-field case*, since the crystal-field interaction energy is intermediate in value as compared with the spin-orbit coupling and electron repulsion. This is found primarily in complexes of the first transition series.
3. $V > e^2/r_{ij}$. In the *strong-field case*, the crystal-field interaction energy is large even with respect to electronic repulsions within the ion. The second and third transition series as well as cyanide complexes of the first transition series frequently fall within this category. With such strong ligand-metal interactions, it might be anticipated that the naive point of view of crystal-field theory is untenable here. This is found to

be the case, and these complexes are frequently termed *covalent complexes*.

As was indicated in the last section, the g tensor is altered from its free-spin value by the action of spin-orbit coupling, and this effect is in general anisotropic. The nature of the alteration can best be illustrated by example: Let us begin by recalling our discussion of Sec. 2–3, p. 18, and assume that we are concerned with a single d electron, such as in an intermediate-field complex of Ti^{3+} or V^{4+}. The single d electron could occupy any one of the t_{2g} orbitals in the ground state, so there is a three-fold orbital degeneracy. However, the complex must distort in such a way that this degeneracy is removed in accordance with the Jahn-Teller theorem. One way of doing this is to compress the ligands along one of the axes (see Fig. 5–4a), which we take to be the z-axis. This is known as a tetragonal distortion, and we can readily verify that the splitting pattern illustrated in Fig. 5–4a results. We call the splitting energy of this distortion δ_0, as labeled in the figure, and we assume that $\Delta_0, \delta_0 > \lambda\mathbf{L} \cdot \mathbf{S}$. Actually, there is still at least a twofold degeneracy associated with the ground level, as with every other level, when spin is also considered. This is known as *Kramers* degeneracy, and it is not excluded by the Jahn-Teller theorem because it is not an orbital degeneracy. It can be shown that no crystal field can remove the Kramers degeneracy if there is an odd number of electrons.[1] This degeneracy is removed by a magnetic field, however, and transitions that are within this split Kramers doublet are induced in the EPR method.

The angular momentum behaves in a rather peculiar way under the influence of the crystal field. For the orbitally nondegenerate ground state d_{xy}, the expectation value of the $\hat{L}^2$ operator is $l(l + 1)\hbar = 6\hbar$, which assures us that we are indeed dealing with a d electron. However, it is found that the expectation value of the $\hat{L}_z$ operator for this state is zero. In other words, the angular momentum has become "tied" to the crystal field in such a way that the expectation value along a chosen direction vanishes. We call this *quenching*, and it is because of this that the magnetic properties of many transition metal complexes can be interpreted solely on the basis of the electron spin.

If we now assign α and β spin functions to each of the five orbital functions shown in Fig. 5–4a, and investigate the effect of the perturbing Hamiltonian,

$$\lambda\hat{\mathbf{L}} \cdot \hat{\mathbf{S}} = \lambda[\hat{L}_z\hat{S}_z + \tfrac{1}{2}(\hat{L}_+\hat{S}_- + \hat{L}_-\hat{S}_+)] \tag{4–24}$$

[1] The reader may think that this is a rather trivial result, since he has perhaps by now become accustomed to glibly dropping electrons, two by two, into each orbital— one with α spin and the other with β spin. This is only an approximation when spin-orbit coupling is considered, however, as we shall soon see.

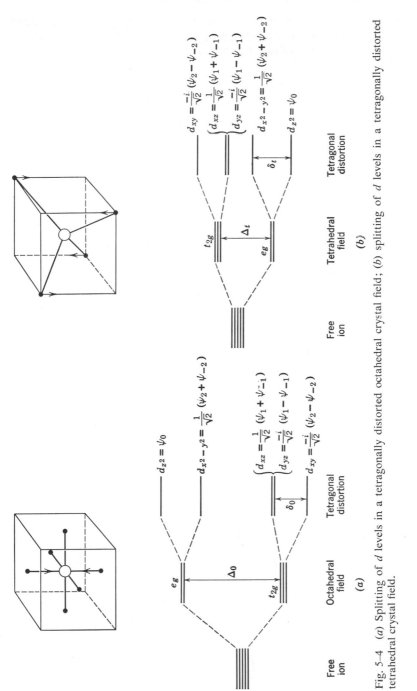

Fig. 5-4 (a) Splitting of d levels in a tetragonally distorted octahedral crystal field; (b) splitting of d levels in a tetragonally distorted tetrahedral crystal field.

135

we find that each of the wave functions of the ground-state doublet includes components of both α and β spin. Straightforward application of perturbation theory (see Eq. 2–18) yields

$$"d_{xy}\alpha" = \left(d_{xy} - \frac{\lambda}{\Delta_0} d_{x^2-y^2}\right)\alpha + \frac{\lambda}{2\delta_0}(d_{xz} - d_{yz})\beta$$

$$"d_{xy}\beta" = \left(d_{xy} + \frac{\lambda}{\Delta_0} d_{x^2-y^2}\right)\beta - \frac{\lambda}{2\delta_0}(d_{xz} + d_{yz})\alpha$$

(5–25)

If the expectation value of $\hat{L}_z$ is evaluated for these perturbed states, it will be found that it is no longer zero. Thus, the spin-orbit coupling reinstates part of the orbital angular momentum which is lost by quenching of the crystal field, as well as mixing the so-called pure spin states.

The states of the Kramers doublet (Eqs. 5–25) are still degenerate, but this remaining degeneracy is removed by the application of the magnetic field. Our former discussions have shown that the energy of a dipole in a magnetic field is

$$E = -\mathbf{\mu} \cdot \mathbf{H}$$

where

$$\mathbf{\mu} = -g\beta_M \mathbf{J}$$

Now $\mathbf{J} = \mathbf{L} + \mathbf{S}$, but the magnetic moment associated with the spin momentum is larger than that associated with the orbital momentum by a factor 2.0023 (see Sec. 2–4). Thus,

$$E = (\mathbf{L} + g_0\mathbf{S})\beta_M \cdot \mathbf{H}$$

where $g_0 = 2.0023$ is the free-spin g value for an electron, and the corresponding Hamiltonian operator is

$$\hat{H} = (\hat{\mathbf{L}} + g_0\hat{\mathbf{S}})\beta_M \cdot \mathbf{H}$$

(5–26)

Taking the field $\mathbf{H}$ along the symmetry (fourfold) axis of the tetragonally distorted ion, it is found, by using the foregoing Hamiltonian, that the split in energy of the ground-state-doublet term is

$$\left(g_0 - 8\frac{\lambda}{\Delta_0}\right)\beta_M H$$

Similarly, it is found, by using $\hat{H}_x$ and $\hat{H}_y$, that the split in energy is the same in these two directions, as it must be for this axial case. It is given by

$$\left(g_0 - 2\frac{\lambda}{\delta_0}\right)\beta_M H$$

We describe these results by an axial g tensor whose principal values are

$$g_{\parallel} = g_0 - 8\frac{\lambda}{\Delta_0} \qquad g_{\perp} = g_0 - 2\frac{\lambda}{\delta_0} \qquad (5\text{-}27)$$

Thus we see that the splitting of the Kramers doublet depends on the orientation of the magnetic field with respect to the ion, and it is this orientation dependence which leads to the anisotropy of the g tensor.

Another example is the tetragonally distorted tetrahedral coordination shown in Fig. 5–4b. Similar calculations in this case show that the low-lying Kramers doublet is

$$''d_{z^2}\alpha'' = d_{z^2}\alpha - \frac{\sqrt{3}}{2}\frac{\lambda}{\Delta_t}(d_{xz} + d_{yz})\beta$$

$$''d_{z^2}\beta'' = d_{z^2}\beta - \frac{\sqrt{3}}{2}\frac{\lambda}{\Delta_t}(d_{xz} - d_{yz})\alpha \qquad (5\text{-}28)$$

and this leads to a g tensor of the form,

$$g_{\parallel} = g_0 \qquad g_{\perp} = g_0 - 6\frac{\lambda}{\Delta_t} \qquad (5\text{-}29)$$

independent of δ_t.

It is possible to carry out calculations of this sort for any assumed coordination, and we see here an obvious connection between optical and EPR parameters. The two methods employed simultaneously can provide valuable information quite readily, which could only be gleaned with great difficulty when either is independently used.

It should be pointed out that the g tensors are sometimes considerably more complicated than we have indicated here. In particular, we are in many cases unsure of the nature of the Jahn-Teller distortion. If the distortion is not large with respect to the spin-orbit coupling, then a simultaneous perturbation by these two effects must be considered. This, of course, implies that there may be a considerable distribution of population between the first excited state and the ground state, so the observed spectrum may be a complex superposition which is temperature dependent.

If there is an even number of electrons, Kramers theorem is no longer operative, but we still frequently obtain paramagnetic ions which are suitable for study by EPR techniques. Hund's rules, which were mentioned in Sec. 3–1, p. 42, are of interest in this connection. It is found in such cases that the spin degeneracy of an energy level of higher multiplicity may be removed by the crystal field alone. This comes about through the zero-field-splitting interaction briefly referred to in Sec. 5–2, p. 126.

A Hamiltonian quadratic in the electron spin **S** was introduced; higher-order terms usually need not be included except in the analysis of S ($L = 0$) state ions.

Let us assume that spin-orbit coupling effects are small. Then, an appropriate Hamiltonian for Zeeman and zero-field interactions in the principal-axis system is

$$\hat{H} = g_0 \beta_M H \hat{S}_{z'} + D \hat{S}_z^2 + E(\hat{S}_x^2 - \hat{S}_y^2) \tag{5-30}$$

where z' is the axis of the static field **H**. **D** is taken to be a traceless tensor, so that the two parameters D and E are sufficient to define a completely anisotropic zero-field splitting; $E = 0$ in the axial case.

We observe, first of all, that if $D, E \ll g_0 \beta_M H$, the zero-field splitting is but a small perturbation. In this case, all the transitions, with the exception of that corresponding to $M = \pm \frac{1}{2}$, are slightly shifted (note the analogy with the quadrupole effect on NMR spectra discussed in Sec. 4–2). Thus, if there are weak crystalline fields, we could expect to see a relatively unperturbed resonance corresponding to the free-spin g value.

Now in the other limit, i.e., $g_0 \beta_M H \ll D$ or E, we may solve for the energy levels of the zero-field splitting and then treat the Zeeman term as a perturbation. If $E = 0$, we obtain a resonance which ranges from a g value of g_0 at z' parallel to z, to a value of $2S + 1$ for z' perpendicular to z. For the $D = 0$ case, we obtain in zero field a splitting of the energy levels into pairs, the exact nature of which depending on S. The splitting of these pairs by the magnetic field can lead to sharp resonances which are independent of the orientation and far removed from the free-spin g value [Castner et al. (Ref. 11) have reported an excellent example—Fe^{3+} in glass.]

We are seldom lucky enough to find one of these limiting cases in practice, but occasionally it does happen. In general, the terms must be dealt with simultaneously with a concomitant increase in complexity. The important point is that by such an analysis, we can gain some information about the relative importance of the various interactions. If D or E is large, i.e., in the strong-field case, the quenching will probably be nearly complete and our assumption that $g = g_0$ is a good one. Then, if $D \gg E$, the field is axial to a good degree of approximation, whereas if $E \geqslant D$, we are assured that the ion site is of quite low symmetry. There is no zero-field splitting in cubic fields to this degree of approximation.

Such information as this is obviously very useful as an aid to our understanding of much of chemistry. It is only fair to say, however, that although we can always infer values of the spin Hamiltonian from a known chemical environment, the converse is not true. We can certainly make some general statements regarding the nature of the site, but an unambiguous determination is not possible.

We now need to say a few words about the hyperfine coupling interactions which endow EPR spectra with some of their more interesting features. As pointed out in Sec. 5–2, p. 126, these come about through both classical dipolar interactions and Fermi contact interactions. The former is straightforward enough, but the latter requires some explanation. We think of the electrons which exhibit the paramagnetic effects in transition metal complexes as occupying d orbitals. Since these orbitals have a node at the nucleus, they obviously do not provide for contact coupling.

Two mechanisms have been proposed to explain the contact-coupling effect. The first involves configuration interaction. Here an admixture of higher s orbitals into the ground-state wave function is assumed. It is found that a very small mixing is all that is required to give a sufficient unpaired-electron density at the nucleus to account for the coupling. A second explanation assumes the polarization of the s electrons of the core (i.e., the inner electron shells) by the d electron(s). This is tantamount to saying that the action of the d electron(s) on the s shells is to make the orbitals for the α and β electrons inequivalent, so that the densities of the two at the nucleus are no longer equal. Although each of these proposals has its attractive features, quantitative calculations of neither have been entirely successful, so that the question should still be regarded as unsettled.

Our remarks thus far apply to ions in pure crystal fields, and we now need to consider the effects of covalency. There has been an increasing accumulation of evidence in recent years that ligand-metal overlap is quite significant in many cases, with perhaps the most direct evidence emerging from EPR studies.

There are several ways in which electron delocalization manifests itself, one of which is in the g values. Typically, we find that in place of Eq. 5–27 and Eq. 5–29 we should write

$$g = g_0 - \frac{n\alpha\lambda_0}{\Delta}$$

where n is a factor which depends on the nature of the crystal field, and α is a factor which depends on the extent of delocalization of the electron. These altered g factors can be interpreted in terms of reduced values of $\lambda = \alpha\lambda_0$, which implies that the electron spends a certain fraction of its time in the ligand orbitals. This is because the ligand orbitals are in general of much lesser angular momentum, so there is an apparent reduction of the spin-orbit coupling constant. Detailed calculations do indeed show that the factor α contains molecular-orbital coefficients in such a way that $\alpha < 1$, which is consistent with the apparent reduction of λ_0.

A second manifestation of electron delocalization is in the reduced magnitude of hyperfine coupling to the metal ion nucleus. As an electron is partially removed from a metal orbital and placed in ligand orbitals, a decrease in the coupling interaction with the metal is to be expected, and this is what is observed.

Of course, if the ligand which accepts the delocalized electron has a magnetic nucleus, its interaction with the electron will also be evident. Obviously, the magnitude of such an interaction is related to the amount of time the electron spends in the ligand orbital. There have been numerous observations of ligand hyperfine structure in EPR spectra, which provide our most conclusive evidence of covalency in ligand-metal bonding.

Organic Radicals

There is much we could say about the spectra of organic radicals, but we will limit ourselves to a few qualitative observations. In general, the orbitals involved have less angular momentum than in the transition metal complexes previously considered, so the g tensor is of less interest here. It usually deviates very little from the free-spin value, unless heavier atoms, such as sulfur, are involved. Even then, the contribution of spin-orbit coupling is quite small by comparison.

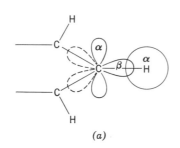

(a)

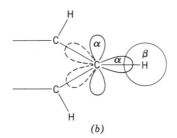

(b)

Fig. 5–5 (a) Parallel polarization of hydrogen electron in an aromatic molecule; (b) antiparallel polarization of hydrogen electron in an aromatic molecule.

Spectra of organic radicals in solution frequently show an abundance of hyperfine structure which can be attributed to contact coupling with the protons. As with the inorganic complexes, we are faced with a paradox. In this case the electron is thought to be either in a carbon $2p_\pi$ atomic orbital, or in a π molecular orbital which is more or less delocalized. This is true of both aliphatic and aromatic radicals, and the difficulty lies in the fact that the protons of such radicals are in the plane of the molecule where the π-electron density is zero. Thus, there is no obvious way for contact coupling to occur.

The answer to this paradox can be given in terms of *spin polarization*, as illustrated in Fig. 5–5. The figure shows explicitly only the orbitals of a particular carbon atom and its attached hydrogen atom. The $2p_\pi$ orbital, which is perpendicular to the plane containing the sp^2 hybrids, contains an unpaired electron which may or may not be involved in the formation of delocalized molecular orbitals. If it is not, then the unpaired-electron density at the carbon atom is unity. On the other hand, if a de-localized π-system is involved, the extent to which the electron can be regarded as associated with any particular atom is determined by the coefficient of that atomic orbital in a l.c.a.o. wave function. That is, ρ_1, the unpaired-electron density on atom 1, is $c_1{}^2$, and ρ_2 is $c_2{}^2$, etc. (It will be noted that such considerations actually form the basis for the construction of figures such as Figs. 2–2a and b.) Thus, by assigning the unpaired electron to a particular molecular orbital, we can determine the extent of its association with each atom by examining the coefficients in the wave function determined by a molecular-orbital calculation.[1]

The electron in the π orbital is characterized by a well-defined spin, which we have arbitrarily labeled α in Fig. 5–5. The electron in the sp^2 orbital bonded to the hydrogen atom can be chosen as either α or β, but the spin of the hydrogen electron will be fixed by this choice, since an electron-pair bond is involved and the Pauli principle is operative. The $2p_\pi$ and sp^2 orbitals are orthogonal so the exclusion principle does not apply to this combination, but the parallel arrangement is slightly preferred by Hund's rule. This preferential orientation transfers a small amount of unpaired-electron density to the proton, and since the valence electron involved here occupies a $1s$ orbital, contact coupling can occur.

Theoretical work by several persons, notably McConnell, has indicated a linear relationship between the contact coupling constant and the unpaired-electron density at the directly bonded carbon atom. This we will represent as

$$A_i = Q\rho_i \qquad (5\text{–}31)$$

The magnitude of the constant Q can be determined by the study of any of a number of compounds. The benzene negative ion, for example, shows a seven-line spectrum, as illustrated in Fig. 5–6. These hyperfine components are the result of coupling to six equivalent protons. Since the observed spacing is 3.75 gauss, Q is $6 \times 3.75 = 22.5$ gauss; that is, unit unpaired density at a given carbon atom position would lead to a 22.5-gauss splitting by the directly bonded proton. Other radicals lead to similar values, and it is by now firmly established that Q is in the range of about 22 to 30 gauss in all cases.[1] This linear relationship provides a

---

[1] Everything we say here could of course be put in valence-bond terms as well.

very valuable link between the theoretically obtained unpaired electron density, ρ_i, and the experimentally obtained coupling constant, A_i.

As we previously mentioned, the range of applicability of EPR is not nearly as broad as NMR, but still a wide variety of species are amenable to study. Many compounds which could equally well be classified with inorganic applications have been studied. Organometallic compounds in general have been of interest, and in particular, the transition metal complexes of such biologically interesting complexing agents as porphyrin and its derivatives have been studied a great deal, with the view of de-

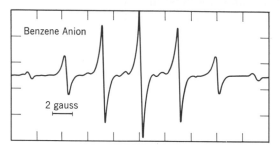

Fig. 5–6 Derivative EPR spectrum of benzene anion radical. [Reproduced by permission from A. Carrington, *Quart. Rev.*, **17**, 67 (1963).]

termining both the nature of the metal-ligand bond and the effect of such bond formation on the electron distribution in the ligand. Biochemistry has also benefited by the study of transient radicals occurring in enzyme reactions, not to mention the identification of the radicals formed by the irradiation of simple amino acids and other compounds closely related to natural products.

Some aliphatic radicals have been studied, but for the most part they are very reactive and of such short lifetime that special techniques are required. Aromatic radicals are generally more stable and have attracted more attention. C^{13} couplings have been of some interest, but most of the work has centered around the determination of the molecular-orbital structure of various homo- and heterocyclic aromatic radicals. The

[1] Some small variations are attributed to differences in the effectiveness of the transfer of unpaired-electron density to the proton because of differences in the *total* electron density at the carbon atom. A comparison of the EPR spectra of the aromatic cation and anion radicals of even, alternate hydrocarbons shows this quite clearly. The splitting pattern is the same, because the cation and anion radicals of a particular compound have unpaired electrons in the highest bonding and lowest antibonding orbitals respectively, and the coefficients in the wave functions of these two orbitals differ only in sign, so the distribution is the same (see, for example, the orbitals of benzene given in Sec. 2–3, p. 16) and the splitting patterns are identical. The magnitude of these two splittings is slightly different however.

procedure is usually one of determining electron densities experimentally (through the McConnell equation), and seeing how well these correlate with those calculated with various models.

Experience has shown that, if we wish to expend sufficient effort, reasonable agreement between calculated and experimental densities can be achieved. The amount of effort required is frequently prohibitive in larger systems, however, and it is often useful to rely on simple models and calculations for a qualitative understanding where possible. As an example, it has been found that the qualitative changes in the EPR spectra of benzenoid radicals upon substitution can be quite nicely explained in simple terms as follows: Referring to Sec. 2–3, p. 16, we have a set of molecular orbitals describing the electron density in each of the π-electron states of benzene. These orbitals are not in the most convenient form, however. Since we wish to classify substituents as either electron attracting or repelling, it will be convenient to use a set of orbitals in which the electron density at a particular proton position is either a maximum or a minimum. Any linear combination of Ψ_2 and Ψ_3 is an acceptable wave function, owing to the degeneracy of these states, and the same is true of Ψ_4 and Ψ_5. Thus we choose the set of orbitals,

$$\Psi'_1 = \frac{1}{\sqrt{6}} (\varphi_1 + \varphi_2 + \varphi_3 + \varphi_4 + \varphi_5 + \varphi_6)$$

$$\Psi'_2 = \frac{1}{\sqrt{4}} (\varphi_1 + \varphi_2 - \varphi_4 - \varphi_5)$$

$$\Psi'_3 = \frac{1}{\sqrt{12}} (\varphi_1 - \varphi_2 - 2\varphi_3 - \varphi_4 + \varphi_5 + 2\varphi_6)$$

$$\Psi'_4 = \frac{1}{\sqrt{4}} (\varphi_1 - \varphi_2 + \varphi_4 - \varphi_5)$$

$$\Psi'_5 = \frac{1}{\sqrt{12}} (\varphi_1 + \varphi_2 - 2\varphi_3 + \varphi_4 + \varphi_5 - 2\varphi_6)$$

$$\Psi'_6 = \frac{1}{\sqrt{6}} (\varphi_1 - \varphi_2 + \varphi_3 - \varphi_4 + \varphi_5 - \varphi_6)$$

Figure 5–7 shows the electron distribution for these various states, and the nodal planes are also indicated.

Now in the benzene anion radical, the unpaired electron has equal probability of being in either state 4 or state 5 because of the twofold degeneracy. This leads to an average electron density of $\frac{1}{6}$ at each of the ring positions, as we know must be the case.

We will assume that in a substituted benzene, the interaction is primarily inductive, so that the electron distribution in the orbitals of benzene is essentially unaltered. The degeneracy of the states 2 and 3, and 4 and 5, will be removed, however, and the unpaired electron will occupy one of the set preferentially, as determined by the electron-attracting power of the substituent. If the substituent attracts electrons, states 3 and 5 will be preferred for the unpaired electron, since the electron density is a maximum at the substituent position ($\frac{1}{3}$). The resulting spectrum should in this case consist of a doublet ($A_i \approx 8$ gauss) from the *para*-proton

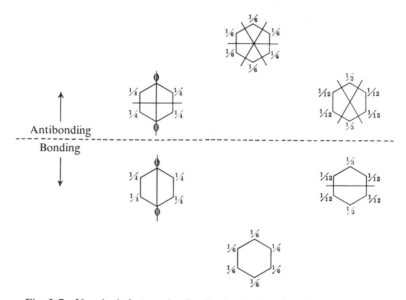

Fig. 5–7   Unpaired-electron density distribution for the orbitals of benzene.

splitting, which is further split into a set of two quintets ($A_i \approx 2$ gauss) by the remaining ring protons (assuming, of course, that there is no magnetic nucleus in the substituent which couples). On the other hand, if the substituent repels electrons, states 2 and 4 become preferred, with the substituent occupying a position of vanishing electron density. Then, the spectrum should consist of a quintet ($A_i \approx 6$ gauss), with the splitting being attributed to the *ortho*- and *meta*-protons. Similar considerations apply to multiply substituted benzene-type radicals, and it is found that these qualitative predictions are quite good in many cases. Of course, better agreement is to be expected by including the substituent in a molecular-orbital calculation, rather than considering only the inductive perturbation as we have done here. However, such observations can be useful and provide some insight into the nature of substituent effects on the electron density.

Hückel molecular-orbital calculations have been quite successful for most organic radicals, particularly for even, alternate hydrocarbons. Some anomalies have been observed in compounds of other types, however. The discrepancies are usually most notable at positions of low unpaired-electron density. The difficulty seems to lie in the fact that Hückel molecular-orbital theory completely neglects electron spin in the construction of molecular orbitals. More complete calculations include resonance with excited states, or configuration interaction. As a result, a certain amount of unpaired-spin character may be attributed to all the occupied molecular orbitals. In some orbitals the spin is α, in others it is β, and these tend to compensate for each other to some extent. Thus, the total *spin density*, which is the excess of electron density of α or β spin, is what is actually required. These refinements increase the labor involved in calculations by a considerable amount, but more faithfully account for the features experimentally observed.

Another noteworthy observation is the fact that the protons of methyl substituents in aromatic molecules frequently couple to about the same extent as the directly bonded ring protons. This phenomenon has frequently been discussed in terms of a hyperconjugative mechanism by which the spin density is transferred to the methyl proton positions, although an exchange polarization, similar to that affecting the directly bonded aromatic protons, may also be important.

SUPPLEMENTARY READING

1. Varian Associates Staff, *NMR and EPR Spectroscopy*, Pergamon Press, New York, 1960.
2. G. E. Pake, *Paramagnetic Resonance*, W. A. Benjamin, New York, 1962.
3. D. J. E. Ingram, *Spectroscopy at Radio and Microwave Frequencies*, Butterworth's Scientific Publications, London, 1955.
4. D. J. E. Ingram, *Free Radicals as Studied by Electron Spin Resonance*, Butterworth's Scientific Publications, London, 1958.
5. W. Low, "Paramagnetic Resonance in Solids," Supplement No. 2 of *Solid State Physics*, F. Seitz, and D. Turnbull (Ed.), Academic Press, New York, 1960.
6. T. L. Squires, *Introduction to Microwave Spectroscopy*, George Newnes Ltd., London, 1963.
7. S. A. Al'tshuler, and B. M. Kozyrev, *Electron Paramagnetic Resonance* (C. P. Poole, Jr., Translation Ed.), Academic Press, New York, 1964.
8. A. Carrington, "Electron-Spin Resonance Spectra of Aromatic Radicals and Radical-Ions," *Quart. Rev.*, **17**, 67 (1963).
9. A. Carrington, and H. C. Longuet-Higgins, "Electron Resonance in Crystalline Transition-Metal Compounds," *Quart. Rev.*, **14**, 427 (1960).
10. C. P. Slichter, *Principles of Magnetic Resonance*, Harper & Row, New York, 1963.
11. T. Castner, Jr., G. S. Newell, W. C. Holton, and C. P. Slichter, "Note on the Paramagnetic Resonance of Iron in Glass," *J. Chem. Phys.*, **32**, 668 (1960).

6

Double Resonance

When two oscillating magnetic fields are simultaneously applied to the sample, we speak of a *double-resonance* experiment. Several such experiments can be conceived. We can use the second field to irradiate nuclear resonances while other nuclear resonances are being observed, or nuclear resonances can be induced while electron resonances are observed. Still a third possibility is the observation of nuclear resonances while electron resonances are excited. The first two experiments are of more interest than the latter, and will be briefly discussed in the following.

6–1 NUCLEAR MAGNETIC DOUBLE RESONANCE

In the usual nuclear magnetic double resonance (NMDR) experiment, a strong r-f field H_2 is used to irradiate the sample while a weak r-f field H_1 induces the transitions to be observed. We can sweep the magnetic field holding H_1 and H_2 constant, or sweep H_1 holding H_2 and H_0 constant. The former is more easily accomplished experimentally, but the latter is preferable from the standpoint of interpretation in many cases. Both can of course be accounted for by a complete theoretical analysis.

An appropriate spin Hamiltonian can be formulated without difficulty; it is a sum of two terms

$$\hat{H} = \hat{H}_0 + \hat{H}'(t) \tag{6–1}$$

where

$$\hat{H}_0 = \sum_i \frac{\gamma_i(1 - \sigma_i)H_0}{2\pi} \hat{I}_z(i) + \sum_{i<j} J_{ij}\hat{\mathbf{I}}(i) \cdot \hat{\mathbf{I}}(j) \tag{6–2}$$

contains the terms previously encountered (see Eq. 4–30), and

$$\hat{H}'(t) = \sum_i \frac{\gamma_i(1 - \sigma_i)H_2}{2\pi} [\hat{I}_x(i) \cos \omega_2 t - \hat{I}_y(i) \sin \omega_2 t]$$

$$+ \sum_i \frac{\gamma_i(1 - \sigma_i)H_1}{2\pi} [\hat{I}_x(i) \cos \omega_1 t - \hat{I}_y(i) \sin \omega_1 t] \tag{6–3}$$

is the sum of time-dependent interactions of all the nuclei with the r-f fields. Because $\hat{H}$ involves time as a variable, the time-dependent Schrödinger equation (Eq. 2–1) must be used in this case. Solutions are obtained in a reference frame which rotates with H_2, in which the only time-dependent terms are those involving H_1, and these are assumed to be weak perturbations which induce the observed transitions.

The results of such calculations are often represented graphically as suggested by Freeman. If we define the parameters

$$\Omega = \frac{\nu_1 - \nu_A}{|J|}; \qquad \Delta = \frac{\nu_2 - \nu_X}{|J|} \qquad (6\text{–}4)$$

diagrams can be constructed of $\Omega = f(\Delta)$, from which the position of every line in a NMDR spectrum can be obtained. The intensities are also conveniently given in graphical form. ν_1 and ν_2 are the frequencies of the H_1 and H_2 fields, and ν_A and ν_X are the resonance frequencies of the A and X nuclei in an $A_n X_m$ system. The A_n and X_m nuclei are assumed to be magnetically equivalent sets, which are coupled by a spin-spin interaction J.

The convention usually followed in NMDR spectroscopy is to reserve the first part of the alphabet for the observed nuclei, and the latter part of the alphabet for the irradiated nuclei. Thus acetaldehyde, CH_3CHO, is an A_3X system if ν_2 is at or near the aldehyde proton frequency while ν_1 is in the range of the methyl resonance frequency. It is described as an AX_3 system, however, if the methyl group is irradiated with ν_2, while the aldehyde proton resonance is observed with ν_1.

We have indicated in our former discussions that spin coupling may become ineffective if there is a rapid reorientation among the available spin states for a particular nucleus. This is because the small field produced by the magnetic dipole is averaged to zero if the fluctuation is sufficiently rapid, and as a result, the spin multiplet corresponding to a coupled nucleus collapses. This can be caused by the double irradiation as well as by exchange interactions. Such an induced collapse is called *decoupling* and it can be effectively produced in spectra in which $|\nu_A - \nu_X| \gtrsim 5 |J|$. If this condition is not fulfilled, the peaks tend to overlap one another to a certain extent and the perturbation of the A nuclei by the H_2 field can no longer be neglected.

Spin decoupling has become a valuable aid to spectral analysis in recent years. Spectra which are complicated by interactions of nuclei with large spin quantum numbers and short relaxation times can sometimes be simplified, and often a hidden multiplet in a complex pattern can be located and an assignment of structure made. Chemical shifts can also be determined with considerable accuracy from the measured difference in frequency $\nu_1 - \nu_2$. It is found that the condition of optimum decoupling in a field-sweep experiment is

$$\nu_1 - \nu_2 \approx \nu_A - \nu_X - \frac{\gamma H_2^2}{2(\nu_A - \nu_X)} \tag{6-5}$$

One very useful application of NMDR has been the determination of

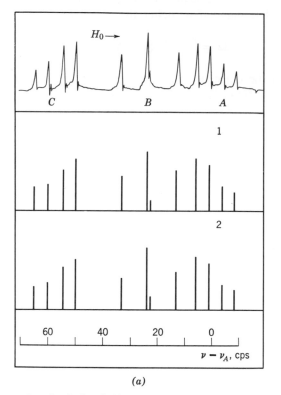

(a)

Fig. 6–1a Observed and calculated 60-Mc NMR spectrum of 2,3-dibromopropionic acid. [Reproduced by permission from R. Freeman, K. A. McLauchlan, J. I. Musher, and K. G. R. Pachler, *Mol. Phys.*, **5**, 321 (1962).]

relative signs of coupling constants. Let us illustrate the principles involved by consideration of a specific example, namely, 2,3-dibromo-propionic acid, which was studied by Freeman, McLauchlan, Musher, and Pachler. Figure 6–1a shows the 60-Mc proton spectrum, together with spectra calculated with two sets of coupling constants. The spectrum is of the *ABC* type, which as a first approximation can be treated as an *ABX* spectrum. On the basis of the magnitude of the observed coupling constants, the following assignment was made:

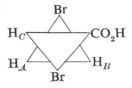

and the two calculated spectra correspond to the parameters (in cycles per second):

Set 1: $\nu_A = 0.0$ $\nu_B = +23.4$ $\nu_C = +57.2$
          $J_{AB} = \pm 9.7$ $J_{BC} = \pm 10.9$ $J_{AC} = \pm 4.3$

Set 2: $\nu_A = 0.0$ $\nu_B = +23.4$ $\nu_C = +57.2$
          $J_{AB} = \mp 9.9$ $J_{BC} = \pm 10.9$ $J_{AC} = \pm 4.6$

It is obvious that a distinction between these sets, which differ in the relative sign of one of the coupling constants (the geminal coupling), cannot

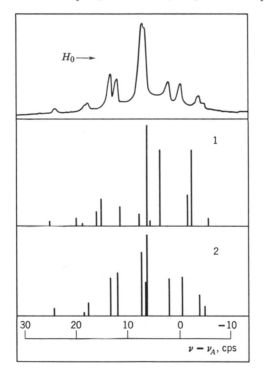

(b)

Fig. 6–1b   Observed and calculated 15.086-Mc NMR spectrum of 2,3-dibromopropionic acid. [Reproduced by permission from R. Freeman, K. A. McLauchlan, J. I. Musher, and K. G. R. Pachler, *Mol. Phys.*, **5**, 321 (1962).]

be made on the basis of the calculated spectra. It will also be observed that the magnitude of the couplings is not very different. This is true in general, because the first-order spectrum is independent of the sign of the coupling constants, and the effect of relative signs shows itself only as a second-order effect.

There are two ways of clearing up this ambiguity. The first involves recording the spectrum at a considerably lower frequency. The spectrum of this same compound at 15.086 Mc is shown in Fig. 6–1b. The calculated spectra were based upon the same two sets of parameters listed in the foregoing, with an appropriate correction in the chemical-shift differences for the new frequency. Since the chemical shifts vary linearly with the field strength while the coupling parameters are field independent, the form of the spectrum is considerable altered, and only the correct set of parameters can account for the observed spectra at both frequencies. In this case, it is obvious that the opposite relative sign for the geminal coupling should be chosen.

Double resonance can also remove this ambiguity. Let us consider the spectrum to be first order, but retain the ABC notation to avoid confusion. The eight lines of the AC parts of the spectrum can be regarded as a superposition of two spectra—one corresponding to the group of

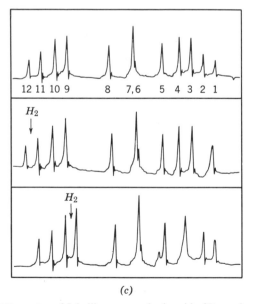

(c)

Fig. 6–1c   NMDR spectra of 2,3-dibromopropionic acid. [Reproduced by permission from R. Freeman, K. A. McLauchlan, J. I. Musher, and K. G. R. Pachler, *Mol. Phys.*, **5**, 321 (1962).]

Table 6–1   *Spin States for Weakly Coupled ABC System with all Coupling Constants of the Same Relative Sign**

Transition	A				B				C			
	1	2	3	4	5	6	7	8	9	10	11	12
Spin states												
A					β	β	α	α	β	α	β	α
					(α	α	β	β)				
B	β	β	α	α					β	β	α	α
	(α	α	β	β)								
C	β	α	β	α	β	α	β	α				

* States shown in parentheses are for J_{AB} of opposite sign to J_{BC} and J_{AC}.

molecules for which the B spin is α, and the other corresponding to the group of molecules for which the B spin is β. Table 6–1 shows the spin states for the other nuclei for various transitions of a given nucleus, assuming all three coupling constants to be of the same sign.

If we irradiate the C part of the spectrum between lines 9 and 10, we decouple the A nuclei in those molecules which have B in the β spin state. Thus, lines 1 and 2 would be observed to coalesce in the A part of the spectrum if J_{AB} and J_{BC} are of the same sign. However, if J_{AB} and J_{BC} are of opposite signs, the assignments would be altered as indicated in Table 6–1, and lines 3 and 4 would coalesce instead. Similarly, irradiation between lines 11 and 12 causes a coalescence of lines 3 and 4 for the same relative signs, or lines 1 and 2 for opposite signs. It will be observed from Fig. 6–1c that J_{AB} and J_{BC} are definitely of opposite sign in the case of 2,3-dibromopropionic acid, in confirmation of the aforementioned conclusion. By similar experiments, J_{AC} and J_{BC} can be shown to have like signs, whereas those of J_{AB} and J_{AC} are opposite.

Triple resonance, which makes use of three r-f fields H_1, H_2, and H_3, has also been used for spin-decoupling experiments. As an example, if H_2 and H_3 are made large and of the appropriate frequency, they can be used to irradiate two of the three nuclei of an AKX system. The spectrum of the third nucleus, observed with the H_1 field, is reduced to a singlet.

As previously mentioned, clear-cut decoupling experiments cannot be performed unless the resonance lines are quite widely separated because of the perturbation of the H_2 field on the observed transitions. By keeping H_2 very small, however, *spin-tickling* experiments can be performed in such cases. Tickling experiments allow a single line of the spectrum to be perturbed, and it has been shown by Freeman and Anderson that transitions which have energy states in common with the tickled line are split into doublets.

Two transitions can share an energy level in two ways: (a) The final state of one may be the initial state of the other (e.g., $M + 1 \rightarrow M$, $M \rightarrow M - 1$) or (b) they may have a common initial or final state (e.g., $M \rightarrow M - 1$, $M' \rightarrow M - 1$). For type (a) sharing, the tickling-induced doublet turns out to be poorly resolved, whereas a transition which shares a common initial or final state with a tickled transition [type (b) sharing]

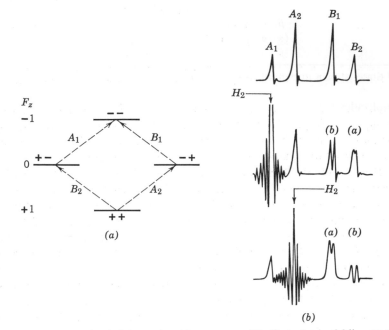

Fig. 6–2   (a) Energy-level diagram for AB spectrum; (b) effect of spin tickling on the NMR spectrum of 2-bromo-5-chlorothiophene. [Reproduced by permission from J. Parello, *Bull. Soc. Chim. France*, **1964**, 2033.]

becomes a clearly resolved doublet. Both types of sharing can be observed in the energy level diagram for 2-bromo-5-chlorothiophene, which is shown in Fig. 6–2a. This is a simple AB system, whose spectrum is shown in Fig. 6–2b together with spectra derived from spin tickling. Doublets of both types are apparent in these experimental spectra. Such information can obviously be of considerable benefit in the analysis of complex spectra by identifying each transition with its terminal states.

Before leaving the subject of NMDR, we should mention that a strong H_2 field causes a deviation from the thermal distribution of population among the spin states, affecting not only the transitions directly involved but also the entire spin system. This readjustment of the populations caused by the H_2 field is termed an *Overhauser effect*, and it depends intimately on the relaxation processes involved. This altered distribution can cause some rather striking effects. For example, referring to Fig. 6–2a, if the relaxation between spin-paired states $(+ - \leftrightarrow - +)$ predominates that between states of parallel spin $(- - \leftrightarrow + +)$, then the decoupled NMDR spectrum will show an inverted absorption (if both nuclei have positive magnetogyric ratios). The alteration of intensities caused by the H_2 field yields information which can be used to facilitate the analysis of complex spectra.

6–2 ELECTRON NUCLEAR DOUBLE RESONANCE

In the electron nuclear double resonance (ENDOR) technique, nuclear and electronic paramagnetic resonances are dealt with simultaneously. The ENDOR method, which was originally proposed by Feher, requires that the EPR signal be (a) susceptible of saturation and (b) *inhomogeneously broadened*. This latter requirement is fulfilled by nonresonant interactions such as unresolved hyperfine interactions with nearby nuclei.

To visualize what is involved in an ENDOR experiment, let us refer to Fig. 6–3, where the energy levels of the simple spin system, $J = \frac{1}{2}$, $I = \frac{1}{2}$, are represented diagrammatically for a given field strength. We assume that the magnetic field and microwave frequency have been properly adjusted to observe the EPR transition between the states A and D, which is labeled $h\nu_e$ in the figure. As we know, the amplitude of the EPR signal is proportional to the population difference between these two states, and this difference is given by the Boltzmann factor if the system is in thermal equilibrium. If the amplitude of the microwave

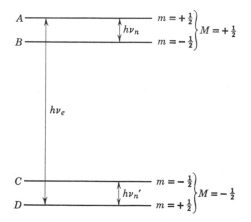

Fig. 6–3 Energy levels for the system $J = \frac{1}{2}$, $I = \frac{1}{2}$ in the presence of a magnetic field.

field is increased so as to saturate this resonance, the signal will vanish as the population equalizes.

Let us consider what happens if we saturate the signal by inducing resonance between states A and D, and then quickly scan through the EPR spectrum. If the time of scanning is short with respect to T_1, the transition $D \to A$ will be missing, although the $C \to B$ transition will still appear. We speak of having "burned a hole" in the spectrum.

We can partially restore this saturated signal by applying a r-f field of appropriate frequency to induce either the transitions $D \to C$ or $B \to A$, since in either case the population difference between the A and D states is increased. Experimentally, this is done through a coil wound around the microwave cavity, which is thin-walled and slotted to allow for the penetration of the magnetic flux.

Thus in the ENDOR method, we monitor the EPR signal while inducing NMR transitions. If the microwave intensity and frequency are adjusted to saturate a particular electronic transition, and the r-f field is swept slowly, a deflection of the EPR output is achieved when the NMR condition is fulfilled. We obtain a greatly enhanced sensitivity for the study of nuclear resonances in this way, since the electronic moment is at least 10^3 larger than that of the nucleus. Nuclear g factors and quadrupole-interaction constants have been determined by this technique. The sensitivity is independent of the size of the nuclear moment as long as it is sufficiently large to produce a set of resolved ENDOR lines.

In addition to the direct determination of small differences in nuclear-energy levels, ENDOR has been used to good advantage to determine the magnitude of small, hyperfine interactions, the sign of nuclear moments, and, in some cases, $\overline{1/r^3}$ for the electron, which is a parameter of considerable interest to the chemist. It has recently been found that ENDOR experiments can be performed at room temperature and in liquid samples. This will undoubtedly lead to many chemical applications which were formerly thought to be impossible.

SUPPLEMENTARY READING

1. J. D. Baldeschwieler, and E. W. Randall, "Chemical Applications of Nuclear Magnetic Double Resonance," *Chem. Rev.*, **63**, 81 (1963).
2. J. Parello, "Couplage entre spins nucléaires en résonance magnétique nucléaire (RMN) et méthode de double résonance," *Bull. Soc. Chim. France*, **1964**, 2033.
3. G. Feher, "Electron Nuclear Double Resonance (ENDOR) Experiments," *Physica*, **24**, 80 (1958).
4. G. Feher, "Electron Spin Resonance Experiments on Donors in Silicon. I. Electronic Structure of Donors by the Electron Nuclear Double Resonance Technique," *Phys. Rev.*, **114**, 1219 (1959).

7

Nuclear Quadrupole Resonance

We have already seen that a nonspherical charge distribution in the nucleus of an atom leads to a quadrupole interaction with inhomogeneous electric fields (Sec. 2–5), and these same interactions shift the nuclear energy states in such a way that the magnetic resonance spectrum is altered (Sec. 4–2). Quadrupole splittings of nuclear energy states are of the order of a fraction of a megacycle to several hundred megacycles. When the nuclear spin degeneracy is removed solely by the quadrupole interaction, and transitions are induced between these states, we speak of pure nuclear quadrupole resonance (NQR). The choice of the name is perhaps unfortunate, since the phenomenon still depends on the inducement of transitions by the interaction of an applied r-f field and the magnetic moment of the nucleus. It is thus within the realm of magnetic resonance spectroscopy. We can of course think of a smooth transition from pure Zeeman resonance to pure quadrupole resonance (see Fig. 4–12).

We can equally well vary either the field strength or the frequency in NMR spectroscopy, but we do not have the same latitude in NQR spectroscopy since the electric field within the sample is a constant. Thus, a spectrometer must be used which makes use of tunable circuits which operate over a sufficiently wide range of frequencies. *Superregenerative oscillators* have been frequently used. A superregenerative oscillator consists of an oscillator circuit in which a tube is periodically cut off by the application of a large, negative grid bias. This cutoff period is made long with respect to the decay-time constant for the circuit, so the oscillations become considerably damped before the tube is activated again. During the on-period, transitions among the nuclear states are excited, and during the off-period, some of the excitation energy flows back into the r-f circuit. Thus, the resonance absorption causes an alteration of the minimum voltage reached by the circuit during the off-period, and this results in a different time-average amplitude which can be amplified and detected. An enhanced signal-to-noise ratio can be achieved by the use of a low-frequency modulation with a small magnetic field ($\sim$100 gauss).

Use is made of the quadrupole Hamiltonian (see Eq. 4–21)

$$\hat{H}_Q = \frac{e^2qQ}{4I(2I-1)} [3\hat{I}_z^2 - I(I+1) + \tfrac{1}{2}\eta(\hat{I}_+^2 + \hat{I}_-^2)] \qquad (7\text{–}1)$$

for the interpretation of NQR data. The axis system used in writing Eq. 7–1 is fixed in the molecule. The gradient of the electric field is frequently such that the asymmetry parameter

$$\eta = \frac{V_{xx} - V_{yy}}{V_{zz}}$$

vanishes. In this case the energy levels corresponding to the foregoing Hamiltonian are simply (Eq. 4–22)

$$E = \frac{e^2qQ}{4I(2I-1)} [3m^2 - I(I+1)] \qquad (7\text{–}2)$$

and just the quadrupole coupling parameter e^2qQ is determined by an analysis of the spectrum. The selection rule is $\Delta m = \pm 1$, as usual, from which the transitions in the column labeled $\eta = 0$ in Table 7–1 can readily be derived.

The $\pm m$ degeneracy of the energy states (Eq. 7–2) is completely removed for integral spins if $\eta \neq 0$. If η is small, however, and can be treated as a perturbation, only the $m = \pm 1$ level is split in the first order. There is a formal analogy between this problem and the asymmetric top molecule which has been quite thoroughly investigated by molecular spectroscopists. The result for $I = 1$ has been listed in Table 7–1.

For half-integral spins, the $\pm m$ degeneracy constitutes a Kramers doublet, as mentioned in Sec. 4–2, and the asymmetry of the electric-field gradient cannot remove this degeneracy. Because of this degeneracy, only a single transition is observed for $I = \frac{3}{2}$, and the asymmetry is not apparent (see Table 7–1). It can be determined for nuclei of spin $I = \frac{5}{2}$, however, from the ratio of frequencies of the two peaks

$$\approx 2(1 - \tfrac{35}{27}\eta^2)$$

NQR frequencies are determined by the nuclear moment and the nature of the compound, and vary over a wide range. Very small splittings are more conveniently studied as a perturbation on single-crystal Zeeman splittings in large magnetic fields. The parameters can be determined with sufficient accuracy by NQR techniques for larger splittings ($\lesssim 1$ Mc/sec), however.

The NQR parameters, e^2qQ and η, reflect the charge distribution for both the nucleus and the electrons and are thus of considerable interest for the determination of molecular structure. In the solid state, contributions from both the molecule itself and from its neighbors are observed, but it is usually found that the latter constitute only a small perturbation. However, NQR can be applied to such solid-state studies as the number and orientation of molecules in the unit cell and solid-phase transitions.

Table 7–1 *NQR Transition Frequencies*

I	$\nu\,(\eta = 0)$	$\nu\,(\eta \neq 0)$
1	$\dfrac{3}{4}\dfrac{e^2qQ}{h}$	$\dfrac{3}{4}\dfrac{e^2qQ}{h}\left(1 + \dfrac{1}{3}\eta\right)$
		$\dfrac{3}{4}\dfrac{e^2qQ}{h}\left(1 - \dfrac{1}{3}\eta\right)$
		$\dfrac{1}{2}\dfrac{e^2qQ}{h}\,\eta$
$\dfrac{3}{2}$	$\dfrac{1}{2}\dfrac{e^2qQ}{h}$	$\dfrac{1}{2}\dfrac{e^2qQ}{h}\left(1 + \dfrac{1}{3}\eta^2\right)^{1/2}$
2	$\dfrac{1}{8}\dfrac{e^2qQ}{h}\quad\dfrac{3}{8}\dfrac{e^2qQ}{h}$	—
$\dfrac{5}{2}$	$\dfrac{3}{20}\dfrac{e^2qQ}{h}\quad\dfrac{3}{10}\dfrac{e^2qQ}{h}$	$\approx \dfrac{3}{20}\dfrac{e^2qQ}{h}\left(1 + \dfrac{59}{54}\eta^2\right)$
		$\approx \dfrac{3}{10}\dfrac{e^2qQ}{h}\left(1 - \dfrac{11}{54}\eta^2\right)$

An explicit relationship of the quadrupole coupling constant to molecular parameters would necessitate an independent determination of Q and q, which is not possible by a NQR experiment alone. q is of course the parameter of greatest interest to the chemist, and it can be expressed theoretically as

$$eq = e\int \psi^* \frac{(3\cos^2\theta - 1)}{r^3}\,\psi\, d\tau \tag{7-3}$$

The radial integration leads to difficulties, however.

In order to simplify Eq. 7–3, we note that the magnitude of q is largely determined by the distribution of valence electrons among the available p orbitals of lowest energy in the atom containing the nucleus whose resonance is being observed. It is obvious that the s orbitals are ineffective because of spherical symmetry, and nonbonding closed shells as well as electrons on neighboring atoms are assumed to produce only negligible effects.[1] The problem thus reduces to one involving atomic integrals, and accurate numerical values for contributions to q for each atomic orbital could be obtained by using self-consistent field wave functions in Eq. 7–3.

A simpler procedure makes use of the experimental, optical fine-structure-doublet separation $\Delta \nu$. It can be shown that

$$eq_{n,l,m} = -\frac{4e}{R\alpha^2 a_0^2}\frac{\Delta \nu}{Z_i}\frac{3m^2 - l(l+1)}{(2l-1)(2l+1)(2l+3)} \tag{7-4}$$

where m and l are the azimuthal and magnetic quantum numbers, and Z_i is the effective nuclear charge which is approximately $Z - 4$ for p electrons and $Z - 11$ for d electrons.

Using semiempirical arguments, Townes and Dailey derived the following approximate expression for the quadrupole coupling constant in diatomic chlorine:

$$e^2qQ = (-1 - S^2 + s - d)(1 - i)e^2Qq_{310} \tag{7-5}$$

It was assumed that the wave function for bonding electrons in the neighborhood of the chlorine atoms can be represented by

$$\psi = \sqrt{1 - s - d}\,\psi_p \pm \sqrt{s}\,\psi_s \pm \sqrt{d}\,\psi_d$$

s is thus the amount of s character and d is the amount of d character. i is the ionicity, and S is the overlap integral.

Equation 7–5, or a minor variation of it, has been used by various workers. Overlap and d-orbital hybridization have often been neglected, but the seriousness of these approximations are somewhat open to question.

Good correlation of electronegativity differences with ionic character in heteronuclear molecules determined by such studies has been found. Gordy has proposed the simple linear relation,

$$\text{Ionic character} = \tfrac{1}{2}|X_A - X_B| \tag{7-6}$$

---

[1] It should be pointed out that an electric-field gradient can cause a distortion of the closed shells from a spherically symmetric charge distribution, and, since they are quite close to the nucleus, this effect is by no means negligible in many cases. The correction for this effect is often written in the form,

$$eq = eq^0(1 - \gamma)$$

where γ is known as the *Sternheimer antishielding factor*. The existence of such corrections must be borne in mind if the equations of this section (and of Sec. 4–3, where quadrupole effects in broad-line NMR are discussed) are to be used for quantitative interpretation.

where X_A and X_B are the electronegativity values for atoms A and B respectively. Dailey and Townes have derived an s-shaped curve for this relationship, for which the foregoing linear relationship is a good approximation throughout most of the range of $|X_A - X_B|$ of interest.

It has been found that experimental values of e^2qQ for Cl in chlorobenzenes can be correlated with the Hammett σ constant, defined by

$$\log \frac{k}{k_0} = \sigma\rho \tag{7-7}$$

where ρ is a constant which is characteristic of a reaction, and k and k_0 are rate or equilibrium constants for an aromatic compound and its derivative. σ can also be correlated with electron densities calculated by molecular-orbital methods and with NMR chemical shifts in substituted benzenes.

The asymmetry parameter η is directly related to double-bond character, as theoretical work of Bersohn shows. Intramolecular effects on η are sometimes masked in the solid state, however. As an example, the NQR spectrum of I_2 has been much discussed because of the observation of a rather large asymmetry parameter ($\eta \approx 0.15$). This large value is undoubtedly caused by the intermolecular forces between the iodine molecules, which lie in planes in solid I_2. It has been suggested that resonance hybrids involving d orbitals are formed which lead to planar bonding and a large asymmetry of the field gradient. Similar considerations apply to the other halogens, although the energy required to promote a p electron to a d state is least for iodine, so that d-orbital hybridization and intermolecular bonding is expected to be largest in this case.

SUPPLEMENTARY READING

1. H. G. Dehmelt, "Nuclear Quadrupole Resonance," *Am. J. Phys.*, **22**, 110 (1954).
2. C. H. Townes, and B. P. Dailey, "Determination of Electronic Structure of Molecules from Nuclear Quadrupole Effects," *J. Chem. Phys.*, **17**, 782 (1949).
3. B. P. Dailey, "The Interpretation of Quadrupole Spectra," *Faraday Soc. Discussions*, **19**, 255 (1955).
4. T. P. Das, and E. L. Hahn, "Nuclear Quadrupole Resonance Spectroscopy," Supplement No. 1 of *Solid State Physics*, F. Seitz, and D. Turnbull (Eds.), Academic Press, New York, 1958.
5. G. A. Jeffrey, and T. Sakurai, "Applications of Nuclear Quadrupole Resonance," in *Progress in Solid State Chemistry*, H. Reiss (Ed.), Vol. 1, Pergamon Press, Oxford, 1964.

Index